NO MORE BUT MY LOVE

No more but my love

LETTERS OF GEORGE FOX 1624-91

Selected and edited with an Introduction
by Cecil W. Sharman

QUAKER HOME SERVICE · LONDON

First published January 1980

© Cecil W. Sharman 1980
Quaker Home Service
Friends House, Euston Road, London NW1 2BJ

Hardback ISBN 0 85245 148 2
Paperback ISBN 0 85245 147 4

Cover and title page designed by John Blamires
The background of the design on the front cover is
from a photograph of the title page of the first
edition (1698) of George Fox's Epistles

Printed in Great Britain in 11/12 Photon Times by Headley
Brothers Ltd., 109 Kingsway, London WC2B 6PX, and
Ashford, Kent TN24 8HH

CONTENTS

Where Letters in the original Folio had a title this has been included. Margin titles from the Folio have been used for other Letters, but where this was not possible the editor has given his own. These are printed in italic. Where the subject is self-evident, to avoid unnecessary repetition, some titles have not been printed at the head of the Letters in the text.

INTRODUCTION

The two names 'Quaker' and 'George Fox' are likely to be widely recognized, and many people, apart from present-day members of the Religious Society of Friends, know that Fox lived and worked in seventeenth century England, and had some distinctive views on worship and moral conduct.

That century seems very distant, but behind its strangeness it looks more like our own than either of the centuries in between. The talk then was of man helplessly sunk in sin and subject to the threat of eternal damnation. Our own time we have called the age of anxiety, of uncertainty and of futility. The helplessness of depression is as crippling as the despair of a lost sinner. The resemblance is not only at the private level. All over Europe were wars and persecutions about authority in religion: about which official church and doctrine everybody in a country should be compelled to obey. Multitudes of sects and schisms battered each other with sermon and pamphlet, and often with harder missiles, about differences in practice and definition which we can hardly distinguish. The quarrels and schisms of today, and unhappily the persecutions, may be called political, but the suffering and the bitterness are the same.

The letters in this book came from the leader of a dissident minority. Some were written in prison, and many were sent to groups of Friends subjected to harassment as non-conformists or alleged traitors against several different theological or state systems. In fact, the book includes a sort of campaign guide on how to survive suffering and win over the persecutors. From this point of view alone it deserves attention, for it records a story of success.

In 1652, could any one have foreseen that the twenty-eight year old religious pilgrim and preacher from a Leicestershire village would survive travel, persecution and plague to end his life nearly forty years later as the beloved guide to a community of many thousands not only in Britain, but in mainland Europe, and in North America?

Fox preferred to work by meeting people directly for talk and worship. Writing was for him an extension of his oral ministry. Yet he recognised the importance of the written word, and encouraged his Friends to explain and defend in letter and pamphlet their approach to life. His conviction that his message was for all men made him eager to see translations and original works in the language of every country which Friends were able to reach.

In the strict sense Fox himself hardly wrote anything. For most of his life he had with him, even in prison, at least one companion to whom he dictated whatever he had to say. His compositions fall into three groups, represented chiefly by the three volumes of his collected works, in the great memorial edition prepared after his death in 1691. The first of these to appear was a version of his *Journal,* edited by Thomas Ellwood from manuscript autobiographies and other material, as is described by John Nickalls in the revised and partly abridged edition of 1952.* The final volume was a very long collection of tracts and pamphlets, called the *Doctrinals,* published in 1706. Some pieces in this are of lasting value, but many dealt with controversies on long-superseded subjects.

Between these two had appeared in 1698 the *Epistles,* formed by gathering together and selecting letters sent by Fox over the years to groups and Meetings, and occasionally to individual Friends. These letters are rarely controversial; their tone is usually relaxed, and their content a blend of the devotional, the pastoral and the practical. They often give us a closer and more sympathetic view of the writer than does the *Journal.* They are our best guide to the message and the personality of this man whose influence has been widespread and long lasting.

Nevertheless they are little known. Since 1698 there has been

*_Journal of George Fox_ ed. by John Nickalls. London Yearly Meeting of the Society of Friends, 1952, rptd., 1975.

only one full reprint, in America in 1831, which was re-issued in 1975. Some *Selections,* prepared by Samuel Tuke of York, came out in 1825, with an enlarged edition in 1848. An abridgement of these Selections was made by some Philadelphia Friends in 1858, and this too has recently been reprinted in America.* In 1937, L. Violet Holdsworth compiled a collection, mainly of the more devotional passages, arranged for use as an aid to meditation throughout the year, under the title *A Daybook of Counsel and Comfort,* but this has been for a long time unobtainable.

The discouragement to their being read is that the full text of the *Epistles* runs to about a third of a million words. This bulk can however be reduced. The style of the time was loose, with many repetitions, parallel phrases and digressions. Because Fox was having his words taken down, often under difficult conditions, as he thought aloud, with his mind concentrated on a single group or immediate problem, there is much material common to different epistles. There are also some general epistles, mainly from later years, which have long sections of supporting evidence made up of quotations and references drawn from every part of the Bible.

The two previous Selections contained up to ninety thousand words each. The present edition is shorter, about one-tenth of the original. Nevertheless I have tried to ensure that every aspect of the worship and thought of Fox is represented by at least one statement of it, and hopefully by one of the most explicit. Those thoughts and turns of phrase, whose repetition shows that they were major features of his witness, will be found more often.

Inevitably some preference has been given to those aspects of Fox which have entered most clearly into the foundations of present-day Quakerism. I have retained examples of material which might well be found uncongenial now, but which was important to the writer and his first Friends, and which is there-

Selections from the Epistles of George Fox ed. and abridged by Samuel Tuke, 1858. Friends United Press, rpt. 1979, with an Introduction by Jack Kirk.

fore necessary to any accurate picture of what was being said during those first forty dominant years.

The Folio contains in its 552 pages over 400 epistles. The last is numbered 420, but the real total is uncertain because there are some repetitions and misnumberings. In this present work about a third have been used. I have therefore thought it clearer to number them consecutively, and to refer to them as *Letters*. The original epistle number is given in each heading and this should serve both to remind readers that the *Letters* are abridgements and to provide a means of cross-reference to the Folio, or to any other volume of selections, for those who wish to use this collection as a starting point for a more comprehensive study.

In reading the Epistles what impresses is not the unfamiliar language—one soon grows used to that—but the very alert perception of principles that remain valid in changing conditions. A short introduction is not the place for a full study of the teaching or practice of Fox. I hope however that the following notes may encourage readers to carry out their own exploration.

Fox treated the Bible more literally than is possible today. His detailed memory of it was notable, and this is shown by the many phrases from the Authorised Version which are quoted or echoed. Although there was no scholarship to raise doubts, he recognized that the Bible could be misread, and that if it were not approached 'in the same spirit as was in those by whom it was given forth' the 'letter alone' would not guide to Truth. He accepted the Bible as history; he used what we now call myths, the story of Adam and Eve, the Fall, the Serpent, the second Adam, the Lamb, as framework for his insights, but the truth of his discoveries in the life of the spirit does not depend on them.

He turned away from the historical churches and theologies. Since all had resulted in enforced inequalities and persecutions they could not be correct. His fresh reading of the Bible led to a few vivid perceptions on which all his life was based.

He held that divine power was to be found in every man, and indeed in all that exists. All men and women were therefore capable of goodness, and, in some degree, of divinity. He embodied this realization in two phrases, 'that of God in every man and woman' and 'the Light of Christ within'.

Friends today are inclined to use the term 'Inner Light' by itself. Fox never did. It was for him that element in a human being which links him with a creative power beyond himself. Further, he identified the Light with Christ, who was for him its supreme possessor. Inevitably he had to wrestle with the problem of the relationship between 'Jesus of Nazareth' and the 'eternal Christ'. The tension between his sense of the divine universality and the particularity of Jesus can be felt throughout the Epistles.

To recognize the creative power working in oneself, to perceive the possibilities it opened up in life and action, and to resolve to obey it, was, for Fox, to be 'convinced' of the Truth; and those who sought to live by what they were learning were 'possessors' of the Truth. He had no use for those who 'professed' religion, but who were content to 'live in unrighteousness'.

Fox could not underrate the reality of evil, for he saw its effects everywhere. Yet he rejected the traditional teaching that men were by nature sinful, dependent on the vicarious sacrifice of Jesus, almost without regard to the way they actually lived. He used concepts derived from the Bible, the First and Second Adam, and the New Covenant, as the basis for his new understanding. (See Letters 36, 61 and 86). He insisted that whatever might have been the case in the past, man since Christ was not subject to sin, and could by his own manner of life achieve righteousness. The first Friends, though outwardly restrained, were notable for the courage and serenity which resulted from the dissolving away of the complex sense of guilt and fear in which many had grown up.

This very Light which brought triumphant power first operated to reveal the evil in oneself. It was 'the Light which shows a man sin'. Hence it provided a basis for morality. Fox had to contend with people, then called Ranters, who claimed that they had private and individual insights which justified any action which appealed to them. And still today there are many who look on their private impulses as a sufficient reason for any desired action. This dead end Fox avoided in two ways. The Light which showed evil made those who were turned to it aware of the harm being caused by their various failings. The problem of self-centredness was overcome by his strong conviction that sins were what affected other people. In the Light there was unity with the creation and with all men. Out of the Light there was all the greed and exploitiveness which brought disunity. Fox therefore held that the perceptions of the individual were to be tested by being shared with the group gathered in the presence of God. Hence his constant desire to see Friends gathered in Meetings, and his fear of the harm that would come if Friends failed to 'keep their Meetings'.

The sin exposed by the Light meant any action which caused harm, whether to oneself, to any other single person, to the community or to the environment. The tests were therefore simple: 'Does it help or hurt?' 'Does it cause happiness or distress?' This basis for morality, akin perhaps to what has been called 'situation ethics', is worth exploring in these days when the main replacement for the fear of hell seems to be the fear of the authoritarian State.

On the other hand, when Fox says that some action is to be 'condemned' he is not thinking of divine retribution or even of a punishment imposed by other people. Their function is to make clear the harm being done, to counter it by constructive responses if they can and, if not, by the 'innocency' of their own lives. The condemnation is rather in the consequences of the wrong conduct on the individual himself and on those involved with him, and in the misery of his own remorse at seeing those consequences. If Fox had been in a position to conceive of ecological damage he would have taken this as an example of the condemnation of a society could bring on itself by its short-sighted exploitation of—to use his own word—the 'creation'.

Fox does not follow the usual Christian custom of

anthropomorphic imagery. 'Father' and 'Son' are found frequently, with warmth but not much detail. The homely scene in Letter 94 is without parallel. Nor does he show much interest in the events in the life of Jesus, even in the details of the Crucifixion. His attention is given to his character and teaching. The emphasis is on the 'offices' of Jesus; that is, on his various relationships to us, as 'teacher', 'counsellor', 'comforter', 'bishop' and sometimes 'priest'. These are the aspects which affect people as 'doers and not sayers only' of the Word.

On the other hand such words as *Truth, Grace, Power, Light, Way, Love, Spirit,* are found in every Epistle. Fox clearly turned to them as if he found them less inadequate to express what he sometimes called 'the incomprehensible mystery of Godliness'. The most frequent additional word is 'Seed'. Although this was perhaps Fox's favourite image it quickly disappeared from Quakerism, despite its potential richness as a symbol. Fox usually identifies the 'Seed' with Jesus or Christ, but its origins and usage would repay closer attention. The followers of Jesus are sometimes his 'plants', and once or twice Jesus himself is called the 'Green Tree'.

Since professions of belief meant little to Fox until they were expressed in relationships with other people, many of the Epistles include pastoral and practical advice. The early importance of several matters has however been taken away by historical changes.

One of the most serious consequences of the insistence on total truthfulness was the refusal to take oaths, a stand strengthened by the belief that Jesus had forbidden them. Oaths were at that time administered as tests of loyalty to the State, and a refusal to swear brought imprisonment or confiscation of property. Oaths were also sometimes demanded as a trick to remove an unwelcome preacher or destroy a neighbour.

Dress and social courtesies in the Stuart period were extremely elaborate, and were used for show and for maintaining artificial social distinctions. There was therefore good ground for rejecting this form of extravagance and insincerity, even if the consequence was social scorn or much rougher handling. Music and the arts were also condemned, though the actual references suggest that Fox had in mind what he would mainly have heard, silly or bawdy songs, or psalms sung without thought for their meaning.

These testimonies were relevant in their own time but their sequels were unfortunate. Later generations of Quakers wasted energy on avoiding everyday dress merely to maintain an expensive and artificial 'simplicity', whilst an undiscriminating indifference to the arts has been overcome only in the present century.

Several letters examine the use of force, not primarily in conditions of national war but as an aspect of law and order, especially in areas of new settlement where the settlers had to provide for their own security. Letter 108 shows Fox examining the problems which could arise. In this and other Letters 'Blacks and Indians' are mentioned, though without a direct condemnation of slavery. This was to come later when Friends grasped the implications of teaching like that in Letters 69 or 115, and when slavery became more organised and more cruel.

Fox unwaveringly asserted the complete equality of men and women in church and society. It may therefore seem strange that he should be found asking for the setting up of separate men's and women's Meetings. Since however it was widely held that in ministry and business women needed the presence of a man to make valid their doings, he considered their full independence could be best demonstrated by separate Meetings. These also enabled women to gain and exercise administrative skills, and so prove their capabilities. Unfortunately in later Quakerism these considerations were lost, and the separate Meetings continued as a dead tradition for a long time before their abolition. Even more unfortunately, in many areas of life, and in many countries, the equality of women taken for granted by the first Quakers has still to be won.

Young people looking at these letters may object to the emphasis on obedience in children's upbringing. Fox was writing in a pre-industrial society, more like that of a third-world country today, with restricted opportunities for individual change. Apart from the family and always, for Friends, as an extension of it, their Meeting, there was little social organization. Education, social training, and occupational preparation were all carried on through the family. And at that time households included not only children but domestic servants, workmen, apprentices, and even tutors or secretaries. Such groups were self-sufficient, and their heads had to be careful administrators, carrying responsibilities that are now scattered amongst many different bodies.

The language of the seventeenth century is not that of our own. But different does not mean worse, and with a little care the force of words having unfamiliar meanings can be recognized. Some expressions are, like those of today, a sort of shorthand. What, for example, is 'low'? Do we have to say 'relaxed, open-minded, without conceit or aggressiveness'? Some words have however changed very much in meaning and a list of these is given below.

Carnal: *sensual, related to the body, not spiritual.* The word was used freely, with few of the limited and unfavourable overtones it has since acquired.

Comprehend: *to include, to contain,* in addition to the continuing sense of *to understand,* (with an implied weighing up or judging).

Condition: *spiritual state, social level, rank,* sometimes *way of life, occupation.*

Conversation: *behaviour, way of life as a whole.* Not restricted to verbal exchanges, and often used in contrast to them.

Convince: Discussed on p xiii. The idea of *conviction* or *committal* as in law is often not far away.

Creation: a collective for all things made by God. *The material world, including animals and plants, often looked at from the point of view of their usefulness to man.* Unfavourable when used in connection with people who give their attention only to the material world.

Discover: *to reveal, make known, show,* and only sometimes *find.* Rarely in the present-day sense of finding out by exploration or research.

Honour: *rank, status, respect shown to these.* Often involving a distinction between the real honour as due to God, and a false honour accorded to men.

Justify: a word carrying the weight of much Biblical and theological reference, *show to be righteous, achieve forgiveness.*

Lust: *desire, craving.* Used very widely of any desire, especially when excessive, or showing lack of self-control. Included sexual desire as one of its meanings but was in no way confined to sexual connotations.

Measure: *level of ability, gifts, skill, insights.* Related to the concept of a talent given to a man, which set the level of what was to be expected from him.

Mind: as a verb: *pay attention to, consider steadily, maintain, serve.* As a noun: can mean *attitudes, inclinations,* but note 'that mind which was in God'.

Nature: *character, being, quality,* and not, as often today, referring to scenery or wild life.

Own: *to admit, to acknowledge.* The present day sense of *to possess* is very rare.

Particular: *individual, every single one.* e.g. 'each particular' means *'every single one of you'.*

Portion: *inheritance, whatever is allotted by fate.* Not usually *part* or *share* in a general sense.

Profess: *declare oneself to be a supporter of some faith or view.* Often used unfavourably, with an imputation of hypocrisy.

Virtue: often *power, energy, inspiration,* rather than *moral value.*

World: *outward interests and activites of this life alone; people who give their attention only to these, and who look down on any who give priority to religious or ethical considerations.*

Most of the legal terms found refer to the processes of arrest and committal to prison or to another court. One stands out: *praemunire.* This relates to a mediaeval practice revived in the seventeenth century as a way of removing supposed traitors and other dissidents, especially Roman Catholics. It amounted to a form of outlawry, for which the penalty, unless later remitted, was loss of all rights, confiscation of property, and life-imprisonment.

Local and dialect words are rare, fewer than in the *Journal.* I have left unchanged some verbal irregularities, since they do not blur the meaning, and help us to come close to the writer.

The sentence-flow is that of speaking, not of writing. When Fox says 'Let this be read', he does mean *read* aloud, and listened to. When this is done the force and rhythm of the sentence will bring out the meaning. Many verbs are left to be understood. He did not see the need to insert in all places 'I entreat' or 'My desire is that . . .' Another characteristic is to put an apparently redundant 'it', as if to gather up a concept before going on to his main statement about it. It is tempting to think that the very heavy punctuation reflects the slow delivery of Fox himself, and his copyist's pauses. It certainly does not reflect his own practice, as shown in the few surviving examples of his handwriting.

Since it would not have been helpful to keep the original punctuation, and since the condensation of the text often made it impossible to do so, every letter has been punctuated afresh. In so doing I have tried to strike some balance between punctuation by rhythm and our own preference for marking off logically distinct statements. Some compromises and doubts inevitably remain, but I hope that they will not inhibit understanding.

The spelling of the folio is very uniform, and almost that of today. In fact, the whole presentation of the work is magnificently accurate, especially when the variety of the manuscript sources is considered. Capital letters are however very frequent, marking almost every important noun. I have here tried to restrict them to the great key-words, when these stand by themselves as pointers to the concept of God or Christ. In this matter also it is very hard to achieve consistency.

The folio editors printed as cross headings many titles, some apparently going back to the original manuscript. Most of these are helpful and have been retained. A number of the epistles have an exact date or address, and these also have been included here, since they give interesting clues to Fox's whereabouts, and when we relate the tone of several to the prison from which they came their impact is all the greater.

Present day Quakers have no need to be apologetic about Fox. There was no way by which he could foresee the fantastic changes in thinking and living which were to result from the scientific and technological explosion just beginning in England as his life ended. It is an irony of history that he unwittingly contributed to them. His concern for education and for honesty and efficiency in craft and trade soon led to Friends acquiring wealth and the incentive to experiment, so that eighteenth-century Quakers were amongst the pioneers in actions that were to change the world.

In the troubled setting of his time Fox found a triumphant assurance of divine power, of human worth and capability. The problems that human beings have now made for themselves are terrible and daunting. Whatever the future holds, this example of what could be achieved by a life in total obedience to a vision of the Power and Love of God can only quicken our own courage to 'walk cheerfully over the world answering that of God in every man', and 'valiant for the Truth upon the earth'.

CECIL W. SHARMAN

The children of God are not of this world, neither do they mind only the things of this world, but the things which are eternal; the children of this world do mostly mind the external things, and their love is in them. The one is sanctified by the Word, the other painted with the word.

Be as strangers in the world, and to the world. For they that followed Christ in his Cross, they were as strangers in the world, and wonders to the world, and condemned by the world. And the world knew him not, neither doth it them that follow him now. So marvel not if the world hate you, for the world lieth in hatred and wickedness. Who love this world are enemies to Christ, and who love the Lord Jesus Christ, and have him for their Lord over them, they are redeemed out of the world. The world would have a Christ, but not to rule over them. While the nature of the world doth rule in man, O, the deaf ears and blind eyes, and the understandings that are all shut up amongst them! But who love the Lord Jesus Christ do not mind the world's judgement, nor are troubled at it, but consider all our brethren who have gone before us.

G. F. 1651

All Friends,

Mind that which is pure in you to guide you to God, out of confusion, [where] all the world is. One voice of deceit knows not another, nor none of them the voice of the living God. But, dear Friends, mind the light of God in your consciences, which will show you all deceit. Dwelling in it guides [you] out of the many things into one spirit, which cannot lie nor deceive. They that are guided by it are one. God is not the author of confusion but of peace. All jarrings, schisms and rents are out of the spirit, for God hath tempered the body together, that there should be no schism in the body, but all worship him with one consent. As the power and life of Truth is made manifest, watch in the discerning one over another.

And beware of discouraging any in the work of God. Take heed of hurting the gift, which God hath given you to profit withal, whereby ye have received life through death, and a measure of peace by the destruction of evil.

And all take heed to your spirits: that which is hasty discerns not the good seed. And therefore all mind your gift, mind your measure, mind your calling and your work. But wait all for the gathering of the simple-hearted ones, for they that turn many to righteousness shall shine for ever.

Mind the Light, that all may be refreshed in one another, and all in one. And the God of power and love keep all Friends in power, in love, that there be no surmisings, but pure refreshings in the unlimited love of God, which makes one another known in the conscience, to read one another's hearts.

G. F. 1652

That which tends to peace and unity
is that which comes from God.

2

Friends,

No one is justified, breaking the commands of Christ; no one is justified, living in iniquity, and no one is justified, professing only Christ's words, and the prophets', and the apostles' words, and living out of their lives. And no one is justified, living in the first birth and nature, and false faith and hope, which doth not purify, as God is pure. No man is justified, not believing in the Light, as Christ commands, but with the Light is condemned; for the Light is the condemnation of all them that walk contrary to it. Therefore the power of God mind. No man is justified, acting contrary to that Spirit which doth convince them.

G. F. 1652

Get up and walk!

Friends,

That which is set up by the sword, is held up by the sword; and that which is set up by spiritual weapons is held up by spiritual weapons, and not by carnal weapons. The peace-maker hath the Kingdom, and is in it; and hath the dominion over the peace-breaker, to calm him in the power of God.

And Friends, let the waves break over your heads. There is rising a new and living way out of the north, which makes the nations like waters. The days of virtue, love and peace are come and coming, and the Lamb had and hath the kings of the earth to war, [and] will overcome with the sword of the Spirit, and the word of his mouth.

G. F. about 1652

To Friends, to stand still in trouble, and see the strength of the Lord

Friends,

Whatever ye are addicted to, the Tempter will come in that thing; and when he can trouble you, then he gets advantage over you, and then ye are gone. Stand still in that which is pure, after ye see yourselves; and then mercy comes in. After thou seest thy thoughts, and the temptation, do not think, but submit, and then power comes. Stand still in that which shows and discovers, and there doth strength immediately come. And stand still in the Light, and submit to it, and the other will be hushed and gone; and then content comes. And when temptations and troubles appear, sink down in that which is pure, and all will be hushed and fly away. And earthly reason will tell you what ye shall lose. Hearken not to that, but stand still in the Light, that shows them to you, and then strength comes from the Lord, and help, contrary to your expectation. When your thoughts are out abroad, then troubles move you; but come to stay your minds upon that Spirit, which was before the letter. Here ye learn to read the Scriptures aright. If ye do anything in your own wills, then ye tempt God; but stand still in the Power, which brings peace.

G. F. 1652

To the flock of God about Sedburgh

Every one in your measure wait upon God, who is the true shepherd, and leads his flock into the green pastures; and fresh springs he opens daily. This ye will see and experience. And mind that which is pure in one another, which joins you together; for nothing will join, or make fit, but what is pure. Whatsoever ye build of yourselves will not stand. Therefore wait every one in the measure which God has given you; and none of you be sayers only, but doers of the word. And so, walk in the Truth, and be ye all servants to it, and it will lead you out of the world.

Dear hearts, to that which is pure in you I speak, that God alone may be exalted, and all flesh shattered down. And all to take warning, and not one to exalt himself above another, that God alone may be exalted among you all, who alone is blessed for ever. God hath done great things in these northern parts. Therefore all be valiant in the Lord God; and so fare ye well! And the Lord God of power keep you.

G. F. 1652

'Our worship group must take the time it takes to come to a unity or else we will be pulled apart. It is not a matter of pleasing this one or that one (regardless of statues) but of pleasing the group or finding that in which the group takes pleasure.

A Word from the Lord to Friends

All Friends, that are grown up in the Life and Power of the Truth, see that when ye appoint your Meetings in any open place, in the fields, on the moors, or on the mountains, that none appoint Meetings in your own wills; for that lets in the wills of the world upon the life of Friends, and so ye come to suffer by the world.

But at such Meetings let the wisdom of God guide you, that some may be there to preserve the Truth from suffering by the world, that all burdens may be kept off, and taken away. So will ye grow pure and strong.

And when there are any Meetings in unbroken places, ye that go to minister to the world, take not the whole Meeting of Friends with you thither, to suffer with and by the world's spirit. But let Friends keep together, and wait in their own Meeting-place. So will the Life in the Truth be preserved and grow. And let three or four, or six, that are grown up and are strong in the Truth go to such unbroken places, and thresh the heathenish nature; and there is true service for the Lord.

The grace of God, the Father of our Lord Jesus Christ, be with your spirits! Amen.

G. F. 1652

To the Church of God in Lancashire

Friends,

Witness [Jesus to be] the substance of all; waiting in the light of God, and walking in it, then will ye have unity one with another, and the blood of Jesus Christ will cleanse you from all sin, for through it and by it we do overcome. There shall ye witness the Lamb of God, that takes away the sins of the world.

O wait all in that which is pure, to be fed alone of God with the eternal living food! As ye have received Christ Jesus, in him walk, that ye may all honour the Lord Jesus Christ, and adorn his gospel. And be famous in his Light, and bold in his strength, which will carry you above the world, and above all the deceits of it. O, in love watch over one another for good. And dwell in that which is pure of God in you, lest your thoughts get forth, and then evil thoughts get up, and surmising one against another. The Tempter will come to you, but I say unto you, in the presence of the Lord, mind the pure Seed of God in you, and the mighty power of God will cherish you up to the Lord God above all temptations. You will feel yourselves supported, and carried over [Satan] by your Father and your God, who is the virtue of all creatures, the wisdom of all things.

G. F. 1652

The example of Christ is to bear all
with love and patience.

To you all, my dear Friends, who have tasted of the immediate working power of the Lord, and do find an alteration in your minds, and do see whence virtue doth come, and strength, which draws you in love to forsake the world, and hath turned your minds within, which see your houses foul; to you all, I say, wait upon God in that which is pure. Though you see little, and know little, and have little, and your own unworthiness, it is the Light that discovers all this, and the love of God to you, and it is that which is immediate, but the dark understanding cannot comprehend it. So, wait upon God in that which is pure, in your measure, and stand still in it every one, to see your Saviour, to make you free from that which the Light doth discover to you to be evil.

Rejoice, ye simple ones, and meet and wait together to receive strength from the Lord God, and in departing from sin and evil ye will be able to speak to the praise of the Lord.

And meeting and waiting in his power, which ye have received, in it all improve your measure that God hath given you; for ye never improve your measure, so long as ye rely upon any visible thing without you, but when ye come alone to wait upon God, ye shall have every one a reward according to your deserts, and every one your penny, who are called into the vineyard to labour. Therefore be faithful to God, and mind that which is committed to you. So God Almighty bless, guide and prosper you unto his kingdom, where there is no tribulation.

G. F. 1652

Dear and tender Friends,

My love is to you all in the truth of God, and my prayers and soul's desire is to God, that ye may all be kept in the simplicity of the truth in Christ Jesus, growing up in the power of his resurrection, to be made conformable to his death, and have fellowship with him in his sufferings, that your hearts may be knit together in love, and in one spirit to God, and be kept out of all the world's evil customs, fashions, words, works, manners, ordinances and commands.

See, if you do find something in your understandings made manifest, which is eternal, to guide your minds out of all external things, which wither away. The Light within, which doth convince thee, it will show thee when the mind goeth forth, and show thee the daily cross, which is to crucify the carnal mind. Therefore give not way to your wills, nor busy yourselves nor minds with needless and careless words, or such things, for they will draw your minds from God, but keep within. For the measure is within, and the pearl is within you, and the word of God is within you, and ye are the temples of God. And God has said, he will dwell in you, and walk in you. What need ye go to the idols' temples without [=outside] you? The true church, (the saints), is in God, but the imitation of the church is in the world, without God. For God is a spirit, and he that worships him must worship him in spirit and in truth. And ye that know God, dwell in the Truth, and tread upon the deceit; for God will be glorified alone: to whom be glory and honour for ever!

G. F. 1652

Do not dispair in being shown
Sin within you - that is the first
Step toward its removal.
Awaren then means to remove.

9

To all my dear Brethren,

The Light is but one, which leads out of darkness and the dark world, into the world which is without end. Therefore, all Friends and Brethren in the eternal truth of God, walk in it up to God, and be not sayers only, nor backsliders; for the backslider is a sayer, and not a doer, and there ariseth ambition, pride and presumption. But dwell in the pure Light, which God hath made manifest to you in your understanding, and turn your minds to him, and walk as children of the Light and the Day, and be not drunken in anything, nor run to extremes in anything, but be moderate and patient. Wait for the presence of the Great God, and our Lord and Saviour Jesus Christ, and be not so childish as to be tossed with men's words without life.

But ye all, in whom the immortal Seed is brought to light, who are raised up to sit in heavenly places with Christ Jesus, let your light so shine before men that they may glorify your Father which is in heaven. All loving the Light, ye love the one thing which gathers your hearts together to the Fountain of Light and Life, and walking in it, ye have unity one with another, and the blood of Christ cleanseth you from all sin. The knowledge of the letter, which you formerly got into your notions and comprehensions, the dark mind gave dark meanings to it, and so kept you in the broad way; but now wait all, to have the same Spirit manifested in your understandings which was in them which gave forth the Scriptures, who were come out of the broad way, holy men of God, who had escaped the pollutions of the world. And if every particular of you know not a Principle within, which is of God, to guide you to wait upon God, ye are still in your own knowledge; but waiting all upon God in that which is of God, ye are kept open to receive the teachings of God. And the pure wisdom and knowledge is that which comes from above, which is to know God, and Jesus Christ, the Way, which is hidden from the world. And dwelling in that which is pure, up to God, it commands your own reason to keep silent, and to cast your own thoughts out; and dwelling in that which is pure, it discovereth all this. So, dwelling in the Spirit, it keepeth all your hearts to God: to whom be all praise, honour, and glory for ever!

G. F.

From Judge Fell's in Lancashire, the 31st of the 11th month, 1652.

LETTER 12 ⁖ Ep. 24

To all Friends everywhere

Dwell in the Truth, and walk in the love of the Truth, in patience; and every one in your measure keep your habitations and learn that good lesson of Jesus Christ, to be low and meek in heart, giving no occasion to the Adversary by evil-doing. Walk all honestly and uprightly, and ye will be bold as lions, resisting the wicked with your spiritual weapons, not by bloody hands, as the wicked are rending and tearing the just that dwell in the Truth.

O Friends, dwell in the fear of the Lord, that your minds run not out into vanity and lightness, that the world may not take occasion, and the Truth suffer. But keep every one your habitation, where God hath called you, and take heed of deceit, and form nothing in your own wills or minds, but grow up in the inner man, as trees of righteousness which the Lord hath planted, growing up in wisdom and understanding to do the will of God and not your own wills.

All Friends, mind that which is eternal, which gathers your hearts together up to the Lord, and lets you see that ye are written in one another's heart. Meet together everywhere, growing up in the spirit to the Lord, the Fountain of Life, the head of all things, God blessed for ever! Let not hard words trouble you, nor fair speeches win you, but dwell in the power of Truth, in the mighty God. For God hath raised up his own Seed in his saints, which Seed Christ is but one in all, and spreads over all, and throughout all, and we are now through him come to have dominion over the Evil-one.

In that which is raised up in us, which trampleth upon the earthly dark Power, have we unity with God, and fellowship with his Son, and unity one with another. Our life is hid, and our happiness, joy and delight hid from all who are ruled by the Prince of the air, from whose dominion we are redeemed by the only redeemer Christ Jesus. Our unity and fellowship with vain man is lost; all his profession is now found to be deceit, and in all his fairest pretences lodgeth cruelty, and the bottom and ground of all his knowledge of God is found sandy. Being brought off from that foundation, and having suffered the loss of all which seemed beautiful upon the sand, we do declare against that bottom and foundation, by the power of God, in that Light of Christ, which discovers all false foundations, and makes manifest all sandy bottoms. For where the only true seed takes root, there all man's plants and plantations are plucked up, for there the earth in which the earthly plants do grow is broken up, ploughed up, and ripped up, and all things made manifest which have lain hid in it. That mind which doth speak of God, but lives not in the fear of God, must suffer, and pass under the judgement of God. For that mind is earthly, and may talk of God, but not in union with God, nor from enjoyment of God in the spirit, nor from having purchased the knowledge of him through death and sufferings; but from hearsay of him and from custom and tradition. The true fear of God doth destroy that mind, which speaks of him but doth not live in his fear. And that mind is raised up which doth abide in his fear; and this is acceptable sacrifice, which is pure, clean, holy, and without spot.

G. F. 1653

12

To Friends in the Truth

Friends,

The love of God is to you; the springs are opening, and the plants are refreshing with the living waters. Now Friends, walk in the Truth, as ye have received it. Which Light walking in, it will bring you to receive Christ, from whence it comes. Here is the way to salvation, and as many as receive him, to them he gives power to become the sons of God. And the Son of God is but one in all, male and female; and the Light of God is but one. So all walk in it, to receive the Son; in which Light is the unity which brings to fellowship with the Father and the Son. And the Oneness is in the Light, as the Father and the Son is one, and brings you to where he is, out of the world, from the world. Therefore walk in the Light.

This is the Word, which makes all clean, which is received in the heart, and this is the word of faith which we preach. Therefore I charge you in the presence of the living God to wait in the Light, which comes from Christ, that with it ye may receive the Life; that with the Light and Life, which is one, ye may come to have the Scriptures opened to you.

G. F. 1653

Concerning Marriages

Friends,

All they who do act contrary to the Light, and it hate, whose deeds are evil, and live in strife about words, and have their minds in earthly things, defrauding and wronging one another, they know when they do so by the Light which comes from Christ Jesus. So this Light lets them see and know when they act contrary to it, [and] with this Light are they condemned.

And all that do act contrary to the Light, and do join together in marriage contrary to the Light, this is their condemnation, the Light, which leads to God. But who are joined together with the Light are joined together in God, and let no man put them asunder. Here is the true joining, and there will be a clear testimony unto them, that God did move and command, and join them with his Light among all the Children of Light. And this marriage is honourable, and the bed not defiled. And whom God did move and command, and join together, it was by his power.

G. F. 1653

Friends,

To all you that are enlightened with the Light, that comes from Jesus, to it take heed, which leads into the right course of nature; [those] who act contrary to it go out of the right course of nature into drunkenness, rashness, lying, blaspheming, deceit and uncleanness. All this is out of the right course of nature and destroys it, and is to be condemned with that which leads to the glory of the first body, and leads nature into its right course and right being, which man was in before [the Fall].

G. F. 1653

Dear John,

The everlasting arm of the Lord hold thee up, and break all thy bonds asunder, and set thee upon the rock on thy feet, in which thou may'st know his presence, and his everlasting supreme power. And so, the God of Life be with thee! And pray for thy enemies, for the Lord to open them and their hearts, and see themselves and thee.

G. F. 1653

LETTER 17 *⁰   Ep. 32

Friends,

When your minds go forth from the pure spirit of God, there the image of God comes to be lost, to lust after that which is in the Fall, which may appear like truth in the notion.

So dwell in the Light, and wait upon God to have the image of God renewed, and all come to witness yourselves restored by Christ Jesus into the image of God, and to be made by him like to God, pure, holy, perfect, and righteous. This was witnessed; this is witnessed, and this will be witnessed measurably with thousands, who are growing up out of the Fall. Let not the lust go out to anything which is mortal, to be servant thereto, but mind the joining to the Life: here ye are kept in the image of God. So therefore, dwell in that which is pure and eternal, which guides the mind to God: here is perfect peace to those whose minds are stayed upon the Lord.

G. F. 1653

To Friends, for all to wait and walk in the Truth

All Friends and brethren everywhere,

In the life and power of the Lord wait, and from it none walk, but that to the Light of Christ in every one ye may be made manifest, that nothing may reign but Life itself. And so, all your Meetings in every place keep, waiting in the Light, which from Christ doth come, the saviour of your souls, that his presence in the midst ye may all feel, who are gathered together in his name and power in his Light, and from the world's gatherings are turned. And if any be moved (who are turned to the Light) with the power which comes from him to any service for the Lord, to it be obedient, and ye will see Christ with you to the end of the world. But if any go before they are moved, and so from the Light walk, he is a stumbling block, and is to be judged and condemned by the Light.

Ye believers in the Light, wait in the wisdom, that with it and in it ye may be ordered to the glory of God, that among you nothing may reign but Light, and life, and wisdom and power. The dread and fear of the Lord be among you, and truth and righteousness reign, which will answer the Light of Christ in every man. And all that is contrary, let it be condemned with the Light, which comes from him by whom the world was made, who was before the world was, who lighteth every man, that cometh into the world. Though they believe not in it, yet ye may answer the Light in every man, though it be to their condemnation.

Friends, in wisdom walk, that ye may every one adorn what ye profess, that the measure of God's spirit in every one ye may answer. And know the Lord to guide your understandings, and let his wisdom be justified by you all, and ye in the measure of the spirit of God in unity kept, that ye may see righteousness spring and flourish among you, and no deceit stand. Therefore in that which is eternal dwell, as in a royal priesthood, in that which comes from him by whom the world was made who to all your souls is a friend.

So the Lord God Almighty preserve and keep you all, that in his life, dread and power ye may be preserved.

G. F. 1653

To Friends in the Ministry

Stand up, ye prophets of the Lord, for the Truth upon the earth; quench not your prophecy, neither heed them that despise it, but in that stand which brings you through to the end. Heed not the eyes of the world, but answer that in them all which they have closed their eye to, that ye may to them tell of things to come, answering that of God in them.

And ye daughters, to whom it is given to prophesy, keep within your own measure, seeing over that which is without, answering that of God in all. And despise not the prophecy; keep down that nature that would, which is the same as that which acts contrary to that of God in them. Neither be lifted up in your openings and prophecies, lest ye depart from that which opened. When the Spirit is quenched, then cannot ye try all things, then cannot ye hold fast that which is good; the Spirit is it, that proves all things.

G. F. 1653

Friends,

Dwell in the Life, that with it ye may see the Father of life, and in the Light which comprehends the world's wisdom. To you, my brethren, who dwell in the Light, which is the condemnation of the world, and of all the deceivers who are turned from the Light, it is not possible that those deceivers should deceive you, who are the elect, who dwell in the Light which comprehends the world. I do charge you all, dwell in what ye speak and profess, and none to profess what he does not dwell in; and none to profess what he is not; a sayer and not a doer.

God Almighty bless you, and prosper his work, that to the Light in all consciences ye may be made manifest, to the measure of God, which is pure, which is given to every one, that with it all may see what is contrary to God.

G. F. 1653

To Friends, concerning the Light

To all Friends everywhere, scattered abroad,

In the Light dwell, which which comes from Christ, that with it ye may see Christ, your saviour, that ye may grow up in him, for they who are in him are new creatures.

'I am the Light of the world', saith Christ, and he doth enlighten every one that cometh into the world, and he that loves the Light, and walks in the Light receives the light of life. The world hates the Light, and deceivers are turned from the Light. Therefore they oppose it, and some of them call it a natural conscience; and such put the letter for the Light. [But] the Light shall bring every tongue to confess, and every knee to bow; when the judgements of God come upon them it shall make them confess that the judgements of God are just.

G. F. 1653

To all my dear Brethren, the flock of God every where,

Keep together in the Power up to God, and none be discouraged or disheartened at the enemies without, but be bold all in the power of Truth, triumphing over the world. Hold your freedom, that ye may be armed with wisdom, and furnished against your enemies, who are wiser in their generation than the children of Light. But the wisdom of the Most High is spreading, and making itself manifest in your hearts. And waiting in that which is pure, it will lead you into that which was before the world was, before the false worship was, and before the outward temple was, and the false prophets and hirelings. Therefore every one keep your habitation, abide the trial, and stand fast in your freedom, as far as Christ hath made you free: free from man's will and commandments, free from the fashions and lusts of the world. And to you that cannot witness this, wait, and mind the pure, and then the burden will be easy, and wait for redemption and salvation to make it so.

And Friends every where, meet together, treading and trampling all the deceit under your feet; and watch over one another in that which is eternal, and see every one that your words be from the eternal Life. And ye that are led forth to exhort, or to reprove, do it with all diligence, taking all opportunities, reproving that which devours the creation, and thereby destroys the very human reason, for the Truth doth preserve every thing in its place.

And in your Meetings wait upon the Lord, and take heed of forming words, but mind the Power. So the Lord God of power be with you all, my dear hearts! I am with you in the spirit, and in the love of your God, your Father and mine. The love of God is love past knowledge, which bears all things, endures all things, hopes all things, envieth not, thinketh no evil. And the love of God is the ground of all true love in your hearts.

And beware of speaking in the presence of the Lord, except your words be from the eternal Life, the eternal word of God, else it doth not profit nor build up. So, God Almighty be with you in your Meetings, that ye may see him to be your head, king and lord over all.

G. F. 1653

LETTER 23 ··   Ep. 45

Now, to all dear ones, the same Seed, which is Christ, the same Spirit is now manifest, as ever was; the same world is now, as ever was; the same temptations, and the same devil, and the same vain worship of the world, twining into another form and colour. And Jesus Christ is the way, the truth, and the life; the door that all must pass through, and he it is that opens it, the same Christ yesterday, today and forever.

So, examine yourselves, and see if ye have fellowship with Christ in his sufferings, and to be brought to be conformable to him in his death, and to have fellowship with him in his temptations and reproaches, and buffetings and scornings, and the contradiction of sinners, and to be spit upon, as he was. And he that hath fellowship with him in his sufferings shall have fellowship with him in his glory.

Now to all you, who are convinced, and have your understandings enlightened, and the worship of the world doth appear to you to be contrary to the worship of God and Christ in spirit, and all the prophets and apostles, who worshipped the living God in newness of life, give not way to the lazy dreaming mind, for it enters into temptations. So there thou wilt be tempted to despair, and the Devil there gets power upon thee. And then thou judgest with evil thoughts, and he will come to tempt thee from God's worship to the false worship [for fear] thou wilt lose thy credit, or good name, or thy place, or thy authority. And then, though thou hast the praise of the world, yet, disobeying that which should have led thee into the kingdom of God, thy latter end will be worse than thy beginning.

G. F. 1653

All Friends everywhere,

A measure of the living Spirit and Power being known in every one, with it ye are kept diligent, quick, and lively, to walk in the Life that redeems, and gives an entrance into rest. Therefore every one of you know a measure of that Spirit which exerciseth meekness, truth and faithfulness in you, that ye may all know what it is to follow the Lamb, with joy and peace in your minds.

Take heed, that none of you walk by imitation of others only, for though the way they walk in be good to them who are in the Light, yet thou art in darkness and knowest it not, nor canst ever receive any strength from God to carry thee on in the way.

And take heed of judging the measures of others, but every one mind your own, and there ye famish the busy minds and high conceits, and so peace springs up among you. And this know, that there are diversities of gifts, but one Spirit and unity therein to all, who with it are guided. And though the way seem to thee divers, yet judge not the way, lest thou judge the Lord, and knowest not that several ways (seeming to reason) hath God to bring his people out by, yet all are but one in the end. This is that he may be looked on from all the ends of the earth, to be a guide and lawgiver. Deep is the mystery of Godliness.

Dear Friends, ye have long been convinced; look for it ye must be proved and tried, not only your faith and patience in persecution by the enemy without, for that many of you have escaped, but proved ye must be with that which is nearer, even a falling-away amongst yourselves. Therefore stand with your minds girded up to God above the world, lest ye run in vain, and lose your crown, which none receives but he that continues to the end.

                                    G. F. 1653

To Friends, concerning judging

Friends,

Take heed of judging one another; neither lay open one another's weaknesses behind one another's backs. But every one of you with the Light of Christ see yourselves, that self may be judged out. Now, all loving the Light, here no self can stand, but it is judged with the Light; and here no self-will can arise, nor no mastery, but all that is judged out.

And take heed, (I charge you all in the presence of the living God), of a feigned humility and a feigned love, and then that to use as a customary salutation, or a formal gesture. So see all your actings be in and from the Light; here ye will be kept clean and pure, and will come to be sealed in the everlasting convenant of God with the Light that comes from Christ.

And Friends everywhere, meet together, that your minds may be guided by the spirit of God up to God. And know the life of God in one another. And therefore all wait, that ye may come to witness the covenant of life made with your souls, that ye are sealed to God with, that ye may all witness sin and transgression finished, and blotted out by Christ Jesus, the new covenant.

G. F. 1653

To Friends, concerning the cross of Christ, the power of God

The Cross makes a separation from all other lovers, and brings to God, and the ground of evil thoughts comes to be opened, and the Cross overturns the world in the heart. Which Cross must be taken up by all who follow Jesus Christ, out of the world which hath an end into the world which is without end; and all the evil things of the world must be denied. For who loves the world, the love of the Father is not in him; where the world is standing, the Cross is not lived in. But dwelling in the Cross to the world, here the love of God is shed abroad in the heart, and the way is opened into the inheritance which fades not away. For God is not seen but in the eternal Light from whence all pure wisdom comes. This treasure is not seen but with the spiritual eye, nor received but with the pure in heart, and by those who dwell in the eternal Light.

Watch all, therefore, and see what ye do possess. For all who gave forth the holy Scriptures, who dwelt in the fear of God, they possessed the Life, which these words proceeded from, and the secrets of the Lord were with them.

Therefore all in your measure, which is of God, wait, that it may guide your minds up to God, and follow it, and not your evil desires; [for] the deeds that are evil, ye know them to be so by the Light.

G. F. 1653

To Friends in the North

All Friends, whose minds are turned to the Light, meet together, and wait upon the Lord, and keep your several Meetings in the Light of Christ, that all your hearts may be joined together, and ye all kept in unity up to God, the Father of Lights. The Lord God Almighty keep you and preserve you, that ye may all see the blessings of God, for the blessings of the Lord are among you. And that ye all with the Light may know your minds kept up to God, to receive the wisdom of God, by which all things were made; that with it ye may come to order the creatures, and in the wisdom of God ye may be preserved to walk wisely.

And that no deceit nor slothful spirits be amongst you, nor hangers-on, getting the form, who speak what they are not. All such I do deny.

O Friends, mind the Seed of God, and the Life of Christ! And take heed of being hurried with many thoughts, but live in that which goes over all, that in it ye may reign, and live in the Seed of God.

G. F. 1653

Concerning the duty of all Friends in the Truth

All Friends everywhere, that have wives, or that have husbands, or that have children, or that have servants; or servants that have masters, or children that have parents, that are not Friends: this is to you that are in the Light, that they that act contrary to the Light and will not be won with the word, that your chaste conversation may answer to the Light in them which they hate. That they, beholding your chaste conversation and good works, the Light may make them confess to your good conversation, and glorify your Father.

G. F. 1653

P.S. Honouring all men is reaching that of God in every man, for that brings to seek the honour of God. For [the honour of men] fades and reacheth not to that of God in man.

The word of the Lord to all my Brethren, babes and soldiers, that are in the spiritual warfare of our Lord Jesus Christ: arm yourselves like men of war, that ye may know, what to stand against. Spare not, pity not that which is for the sword (of the Spirit), plague, and famine, and set up the Truth, and confound the deceit, which stains the earth and cumbers the ground. Wait in the Light which comes from Jesus, to be clothed with his zeal, to stand against all who act contrary to the Light, and are only sayers but not doers.

Arm yourselves like men of war; the mighty power of God goes along with you, to enable you to stand over all the world, and (spiritually) to chain, to fetter, to bind, to imprison, and to lead out of prison, to famish, to feed, and to bring into green pastures. So the name and power of the Lord Jesus Christ be with you! And go on in the work of the Lord, [that all they] who are gathered together with the Light, and their minds turned towards Christ Jesus, may see the Lord Jesus among them, their Head, and they his branches; [and] in the Light waiting, and growing up in Christ Jesus, from whence it came, may bring forth fruit to the glory of his name.

G. F. 1653

LETTER 30 ·· Ep. 58

O Friends,

Look not out, for he that doth is darkened. And take heed of lightness; take heed of the world, and of busying your minds with things not serviceable. O! be valiant for the Truth upon the earth, and tread upon deceit. And keep to *yea* and *nay;* for he that hath not power over his own tongue, his religion is vain. And take heed of knowledge, for it puffeth up, but dwell in the Truth, and be what ye speak. Wait on the Lord: he will perfect his work among you.

He that hearkens diligently to the teacher within, denieth all outward hireling-teachers. He that is made the temple of the Holy Ghost placeth no holiness in the world's temples. There is not a word in all the Scriptures to hold up the practice of sprinkling infants; nor the word *sacrament;* nor to hold up an hour-glass to preach by for an hour's time in a place; but the vain mind doth hold up many things which Christ doth not command.

Earth maketh masters, but let him that ruleth, rule in love. And he that laboureth, let him labour as to the Lord, in love. So let Love be the head in all things, and then the Lord is exalted. So be faithful in all things, and keep from the world's vain customs.

Do not wear apparel to gratify the proud mind; neither eat nor drink to make yourselves wanton, for it was created for the health and not for the lust, to be as servants to us, and we servants to God, to use all these things to his glory. To whom be praises, honour and glory for ever more, who hath created all things to his glory, and so to be used and spent.

G. F. 1654

To Friends, to keep in the fear of the Lord

Friends,

Every [one] mind that which is pure of God in you to guide you up to God, and to keep you in the fear of the Lord, that ye may receive refreshment from God alone in yourselves, and grow up in the inward man, nourished and strengthened by that which is immortal. And delight in that which shows you the deceit of your hearts, and judges that which is contrary to God, and be obedient to that which is pure. So ye will see the Lord God present with you, a daily help, his hand always ordering of you, and as a shepherd always keeping the dogs from his lambs, whom he feeds in green pastures, and waters with his heavenly dew of mercy, who makes them all fruitful.

The cry of want and poverty shall be no more heard in the land of the living, but joy, gladness and plenty. The wearied soul, that hath lain in the pit and in the mire, and lived in the clouds of temptation, and cried out for want of the Lord, shall cry *plenteous redemption,* and say 'God is our King who fills heaven and earth, and the voice of our King is heard in our land', So fare ye well in the Lord! and the Lord God Almighty keep you and preserve you in his mighty power.

G. F. 1654

Friends,

Dwell all in the immortal Seed of God, which is heir of the promise of God; so every one of you know the promise and power of God your portion, and the kingdom of God, and the power of an endless life, and come to inherit it and possess it. And know the Seed of God, that never changeth, but standeth steadfast and distinct from all the changeables. Which Seed endeth all types, figures and shadows, and variable things; which Seed doth not change, which is Christ, which keeps above all the inventions, rudiments, traditions, vain talkers and babblers that be in the world, and standeth when they will be all gone. In which Seed is the power, wisdom and life eternal, which hath the dominion in the life and power, and unchangeable wisdom of God, which is pure and gentle from above. In the love and life and power of God ye are kept above all outward things that have been set up in the Fall, which causeth pride and contention, and strife. So all in that live, which brings you up to God, out of the state of Adam and Eve and his sons and daughters in the Fall. In that power ye will have an everlasting fellowship with God, and one with another. Which power of God was before the Fall was. In that power ye shall ever be together, and know your election, before the world began. So farewell.

G. F. 1654

Always the Light is the Light of
Christ, always. How is it that
we know better now ??

To Friends, concerning the covenant of Light and life

Friends everywhere, to the measure of the life of God in you all take heed, that with it your minds may be guided up to the living God, from whence Light and life doth come, and virtue, and strength and nourishment. To the measure of Light take heed, that with it all your minds may be guided up to the Father of life, that the knowledge of the glory of God in the face of Christ Jesus ye may all come to enjoy. So that in peace, patience, righteousness, and temperance and godliness ye may be kept, and all grow up in brotherly kindness, and be kept from that which causeth strife, and sects, and divisions. To that which is pure and lowly take heed, that mastery and strife may be thrown down, so that the light of the glorious gospel may shine, and that ye may all know it. So, all having a light from Christ Jesus, the righteousness of God, he is the way to the Father, whom God gave for a covenant of light, life and peace.

So feeling the presence of the Lord God with you, ye receive virtue into your souls from the living God, who nourisheth his own living plant and plants. So the Lord God almighty preserve you in the Light, which shows to every one their evil deeds, and reproves for them. This is the true Light, which will let you see the chief shepherd and bishop of your souls, for it is that which restores you to Christ, the bishop of your souls, who is the prophet that must be heard. Therefore wait every one in your measure to know the Scripture fulfilled in you, which came not by the will of man, but was learned of God. Therefore every one wait in the measure of the Spirit, to learn of him, as they did which gave [the Scripture] forth.

G. F. 1654

To Friends in the Ministry

All Friends, who are moved of the Lord to speak the word of the Lord, whom the Lord hath made to be his mouth, speak not your own words to feed the sensual part of man, in your own wills; for there God is not honoured, and wisdom is not justified. But ye that are moved to speak in steeple-houses, or to the priests, (who have not the word of the Lord but the letter), speak the word of the Lord faithfully, neither add to it with your reason, nor diminish from it with a disobedient mind; but, speaking the word of the Lord faithfully, it is sharper than a two-edged sword, to cut down all deceit, and it purifies you that speak it. And the word is but one, which sanctifies all, and cleanseth the heart, and reconciles to God. And the Light is but one; and all being guided by it, all are subject to One, and are one in the unity of the spirit. And if your minds turn from the Light, there gets up pride, and presumption, and then ye begin to strike your fellow-servants.

Therefore all dear Friends and brethren, be servants to the Truth, and do not strive for mastery, but serve one another in love. Wash one another's feet. Take Christ for your example, that I may hear of no strife among you, but walk all in the Truth, and in the love of it, up to God, for there ye are my joy and crown in the land.

And Friends, spread yourselves abroad, that ye may be serviceable for the Lord and his Truth, and trample all that which is contrary to God under your feet, that ye may answer that of God in every one.

G. F. 1654

Note form of original

To Friends at Malton

All my dear Friends at Malton,

Mind that which is pure in you, that ye may grow up in the power, out of the form. And take heed of deceit, and of jarring with one another; take heed of strife and confusion in your minds. But mind the pure life of God in you, according to your measures, to guide you up to God out of the flesh, and all the ways and works of it, within and without. So all walk in the wisdom of God, which is given into the pure heart, that none of your nakedness may appear, and men see your shame, but all wait in the spirit upon God, to be clothed with his righteousness.

I am with you, present in spirit, joying and beholding your faith towards God, which ye have in Jesus Christ, though absent in body. And all Friends, quench not the spirit of God in you, but live in the authority of the Son of God and his power, whereby ye may be kept on top of the world.

G. F. 1654

hum?!

The pacifist in his refusal to fight gives his assent to the suffering of others (assent to the crime of aggression). How does this square with "do unto others as you would have them do unto you"?

To Friends, to live in the power of God, in Christ that never fell

Dear Friends,

All be faithful in the everlasting Seed, in which ye have both life, and power, dominion and wisdom, and clothing with that which is immortal, and the blessing of the Lord, and peace in the Seed Christ, that never fell nor changed, nor will change, who takes away the curse. For the peace is in the second Adam that never fell, Christ Jesus, and the blessings and the righteousness is in him, but the troubles, and the curse, and the unrighteousness and misery is in Adam in the Fall, and all deceitful teachings, ways and worships.

So sit not down in Adam in the Fall, but in Christ Jesus, then in ye will all have life, that was with the Father before the world began. He ends all the types, figures and shadows, first covenant and priesthood, and ways in the Fall. In him live, and love one another, and serve one another in love.

Keep your Meetings in the name of Christ Jesus, and ye will see over all the meetings of Adam and Eve's sons and daughters in the Fall, their confused meetings and gatherings. So in the Life (Christ) live, that none may be as the untimely figs, nor as the corn upon the house top, that is soon withered and gone. But that ye may live in the Seed, the substance, Christ the Life, in whom ye have riches that never fade away; feeding upon the tree of life, whose leaves heal the nations. So, live in unity one with another, that the Seed may be all your crowns. And so farewell.

My love to all Friends in the Seed of God, Christ Jesus, who was with the Father, before the world began.

G. F. 1654

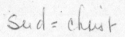

Seed = christ

Concerning Tithes

All Friends,

With the Light ye will see what the apostle meant when he spake of tithes and offerings, and of the changeable priesthood. Now with the Light the changeable priests are denied, and the unchangeable ministry of Life witnessed; and the law that gave tithes, and the commands about them, with the Light ye see are ended. And with the Light God is seen, who was before those things were, and the end of those things ye come to see, Christ Jesus the sum and substance of them.

So all ye that are summoned with writs to answer because ye cannot pay tithes, keep to the Light in you. And so, according to the Light of Christ in them all, speak, that to it their minds may be guided; and declare the truth to them, which is agreeable to that of God in every one's conscience. And declare it to the highest judicature in the nation that ye suffer for the testimony of Jesus, and that ye witness to the ministry of Life. And show forth the substance to them (if you have an opportunity) showing to them that ye suffer for conscience sake. And so over the world all stand, and over all their evil works, and bring all men's works to the Light. And so, if the spoilers take your goods, let them go, and let them take the coat also. And all in the Light dwell to guide you, that to that of God in all consciences ye may be made manifest, that they that imprison you for tithes, and resist the Light of Christ in their own particulars, over them all ye may stand, being guided by that which is pure, that it may lead you to act, that no condemnation upon your actions may come.

The children of Light are one in the Light, and with the Light see the body, and Christ Jesus the head, and are all one in him. Where did any sue for tithes under the first priesthood? But with the Light the primitive Christians witnessed Christ Jesus, the substance of the things typified in the first priesthood's time. To

33

the Light of Christ Jesus in all your consciences I speak, that ye may see what ye act, and that such as are sued for tithes may look to the unchangeable priest, Christ Jesus.

G. F. 1654

LETTER 38

My dear Friends,

Live in the immortal Seed and Power of the Lord God, that ye may meet in that, and in that feel one another. And live in the Spirit in which ye will have unity and peace, and the spiritual weapons to cut down the spiritual enemies of your peace. And dwell in the life and power of God, that ye may have dominion, and come to witness that ye are the heirs of the power of an endless life, and of a world where there is no end, and so in this keep your Meetings. And dwell in the peaceable Seed, which destroyeth that which causeth troubles, wars and fightings.

And living in the Seed, ye will see the everlasting commander, that saith 'Swear not at all'. And the witnesses of the true Seed say the same. The oath did bind to God in the time of the Law and the prophets, but Christ, the oath of God, the everlasting covenant, ends the Law and the prophets, bringeth up to God, and destroyeth the devil, and endeth strife and oaths.

And the everlasting command of the Royal Seed is, to love enemies (which the Jews were allowed to destroy) for ye are all brethren, not ruling in lordship like the Jews and the gentiles, for the greatest shall be as the least amongst you; for the Seed is one in all, and that is the Master.

G. F.1654

[handwritten margin note: But not the military. This is a peaceful message.]

[handwritten note at bottom: Love ≠ destroy]

34

Friends,

In the measure of the life of God wait, to guide your minds up to the Father of Life, where there is no shadow nor changing. As ye do thither come, ye must know a removing and a changing of that which will change; to that take heed to guide your minds, that none be found naked; for who are found naked, they are in that which hath an end, and that causeth blindness. And therefore to you all this is the word of the Lord: in the measure of the Life wait, that it may come to join your hearts unto the Father of Life, that clothing and righteousness ye all may come to receive, and come to feel your strength renewed from the God of all strength, to every one of you according to your measure, and see him that mercy shows. And so in peace live, which comes from the God of all peace. So here the God of love will in your hearts come to be shed abroad, that over all that which is contrary to the Lord of life, who destroys death, ye may reign every one over your own hearts. So that ye may come to know the saints' state, unto whom all things were become new. So in it the Lord God of Life preserve you, that to him ye may be a sweet-smelling savour.

And, my dear Friends, keep your Meetings, and ye will feel the Seed of God among you all, though never a word be spoken among you. And be faithful, that ye may answer that of God in every one. And do not neglect your talents, but be faithful in the power and life of God which ye have received.

G. F. 1654

To all Friends, to abide in their callings

To all dear Friends, who are called, who are enlightened, whose minds are turned from the world's worship and teachers, having your eye to the Light and Guide within, which is leading you out of this dark world, peace and mercy from God the Father be multiplied among you! And so the Lord God of power bless you, guide you, and preserve you on in your way towards the holy City. Abide in that which hath called you, and let the time past of your evil ways be sufficient, lest your minds do turn back into Egypt and the world, and so cause the worthy name of the Lord to be blasphemed. For ye may see how far many did go, and were led out of many things, yet did turn again into the world. So mind your present Guide, and your present condition, and your call, and there walk in newness of life, and not in the oldness of the letter. Walk in the Truth and the love of it up to God, that ye may grow up in wisdom, and improve your talents, and the gift which God hath given you. And take heed of words without life, for they tend to draw you out of the Power, to live above the Truth [in that nature which] will not have peace, except it have words. Serve one another in love, and do not lavish out yourselves without the fear of God; such are clouds without water, which have the words but not the power.

My little children in the Lord God Almighty, this is my joy, that ye be all ordered and guided by the mighty power of God, and know it in one another, and know the voice, and the sound of the words, and the power of them. For words without power destroy the simplicity, and bring up into a form, and out of the obedience of the Truth. And therefore walk in the power of the Truth, that the name of the Lord God may be glorified among you, and his renown may be seen in and among you, and all the world may be astonished, and the Lord admired in the ordering of his people. And take heed of running out, to make conceited ones wise. And take heed of strife in your minds; and if there be,

36

and proud mind

then glory not, for it is the vain mind, and it is not good. And let none seek for the highest place, but be lowly-minded, and bear with one another in patience.

And all who are servants, labour in love, as unto God, for the earth is the Lord's and the fulness thereof. And all who have families, rule in the power and love of God, that love may be Head among you. For the time is coming that it shall be, as with the servant, so with the master; and as with the maid, so with her mistress. For it is one Seed that hath raised them up with one power, out of one death.

So all Friends, this is to you, who know the voice of the living God and know your calling: stand fast, and waver not, lest ye lose your recompense.

And stand in the will of the Lord, and be obedient to him; and the grace of our Lord Jesus Christ, which teacheth you to deny all ungodliness and wordly lusts, that grace shall fill and establish your hearts.

And Friends, take heed of unruliness, and vain talking and talkers, for such are not obedient to the Truth; therefore avoid it and them.

G. F. 1654

Dear Friends in the eternal truth of God,

Whose minds are turned by the Light of Jesus Christ towards God, meet often together in the fear of the Lord, and to the Light take heed, that with it all your minds may be kept up to God, from whence it comes. And in all your Meetings wait low in his fear, that ye may come to know the life and power of Truth in one another.

And all ye, whom the Lord hath made overseers over his Church in your several places, be faithful to the Lord, and watch over the flock of Christ with all diligence. Ye which are strong, watch over the weak, and stir up that which is pure in one another. See that in order all your Meetings be kept. Be faithful unto the Lord, where he hath set you, and ye shall not lose your reward. And take heed of forward minds, and of running out before your Guide, for that leads into looseness; and such [minds] plead for liberty, and run out in their wills, and bring dishonour to the Lord. Therefore all wait low in the fear of the Lord, and be not hasty nor rash, but see the way be made clear; and as the Lord doth move you, so do; and when ye have done return with speed to the place where ye were abiding, and be faithful there. Be diligent every one in your places, where the Lord hath set you, for the work of the Lord is great; and God Almighty keep you to be faithful labourers in his work.

G. F.

London, the 15th of the 3rd Month 1655

An epistle to Friends, that with the Light they may see their salvation

Friends,

All to the Light, which Jesus Christ hath enlightened you withal, take heed, that with the Light of Christ, the saviour of your souls, ye may all come to see and enjoy rest, and the new covenant ye may all witness, where ye need no man to teach you. And this Light shows you sin, and the evil of the world, and the vain fashions of it, that pass away. Therefore to the Light I direct you, that with it ye may see yourselves. Then in it stand, that with it ye may see Jesus from whence it comes. And not to join with your vain thoughts, nor that which doth consult and frame ways: there is the idol-maker, and the image-maker.

G. F. 1655

Friends,

Meet together, waiting upon the Lord, that nothing but the Life may among you reign; and that in life, love and wisdom ye may grow up. And in the measure of the grace of God all wait, to guide your minds up to God. And Friends, I do lay it upon you for to see that in order all your Meetings be kept. So the Lord God Almighty keep you all to his glory, in his wisdom to himself. Amen.

To be read among all Friends at their Meetings.

G. F. 1655

For Plymouth

Friends,

Keep your Meetings, that in the Truth ye may reign, and in the power spread it abroad. And keep in the Truth, that ye may see and feel the Lord's presence amongst you; and for it be valiant upon the earth, and know one another in the power of it. So the Lord God Almighty preserve you in his power to his glory. Amen.

G. F. 1655

A general epistle concerning the priests

All Friends,

In the spirit of the living God wait upon God, to learn of [him] and be taught by him. For now doth the beast open his mouth in blasphemy, speaking great swelling words. Now are the false prophets seen, which through covetousness make merchandise of the people. Now are they seen, which make merchandise of the words of the prophets, Christ and the apostles, and through pretence make long prayers; who devour widows' houses. And now are such known, who lead silly women captive, who are always learning, and never able to come to the knowledge of the Truth, some thirty, some forty, some sixty years. And now are such known and seen and manifest with the Light, that Christ spake of, that should beat his followers in the synagogues, and hale them before magistrates for his name's sake. Yea, if they killed them, should think they did God good service. Which doth them manifest to be contrary to the Light; which all that are contrary unto with the Light are condemned.

G. F. 1655

All Friends and brethren every where, that are imprisoned for the Truth, give yourselves up to it, and it will make you free, and the power of the Lord will carry you over all the persecutors; in that ye will have peace and unity with God, and with one another who suffer for crying against [the false prophets], and for not swearing, and not giving the world's compliments and their honour, and who are suffering for reproving sin.

Be faithful for the life and power of the Lord God, and for the Truth be valiant upon the earth, <u>and look not at your sufferings,</u> <u>but at the power of God, and that will bring some good out in all</u> <u>your sufferings; and your imprisonments will reach to the</u> <u>prisoned, that the persecutor prisons in himself.</u> So be faithful in your sufferings in the power of the Lord, who now suffer by a false priesthood for his tithes, oaths, temples, which have got up since the apostles' days.

So the power, and life, and wisdom of the Lord God Almighty keep you, and preserve you, to finish your testimony to the end, that ye may witness every one of you a crown of life eternal, in which ye may sing praises to the Lord, and in that triumph! And so, be faithful in that which overcomes, and gives victory.

G. F. 1655

That Friends should have a sense of one another's sufferings

Friends,

In the power of the Lord God live, which goes over the heads of all the world, that so in the power ye may witness forth the Truth in their courts; and then, if ye suffer, ye by suffering will get dominion over their heads. And lay down and offer up your lives for one another. And here is the love of the brethren manifest: to lay down their lives one for another. But the love of Christ is further; he laid down his life for his enemies. So dwell low in the Life, that ye may answer that of God in every one.

G. F. 1655

My dear children,

Grow in the increase of God, and know all your assurance in the Lord, and the Seed in every one of you, which the promise of God is to. And be obedient to the just, and in the truth of God walk, and the love of it. And my dear hearts, in the Seed dwell, which gives the victory over the world, and that in the wisdom ye may be preserved, which bruises the contrary under foot; whereby ye may reign in the life of God, to be as nursers and waterers of the plants, that in the eternal power of God ye may be kept, which gives dominion over all, and condemneth the contrary. In which power the Lord God Almighty preserve you to his glory. Amen.

Live in the life of God and feel it.

And, Friends, take heed of being hurried with many thoughts; but live in that which goes over them all.

G. F. 1655

To a Friend

In the will of God stand, with thy own will offered up, as his was, who said, 'Not my will, but thine be done'. And beware of striving in thy own will against the eternal providence and power, which is now working invisibly, cross and contrary to all the powers of darkness. And in the fear of the Lord wait, that thy duty to the Lord thou mayst know, whose everlasting love is to thee; whose blessing reacheth unto thee, if thou be faithful with faithful Abraham, who received the blessing, and to his seed after him. So beware, lest through thy forwardness and rashness thou bring the curse upon thee, and so break thy peace and covenant with the Lord God. The everlasting God give thee faith in Christ Jesus, in whom the promise is *yea* and *nay*.

G. F. 1655

Concerning all such, as set up outward Crosses

Friends,

In the power of the Lord God dwell and live, that over all the world ye may stand, that ye may handle the word of God aright, which is as a hammer, and as a sword to divide the precious from the vile, and as a fire to burn up that which is hammered down, and divided from the precious. And in the wisdom of God wait, that ye may answer that of God in every one; which Light will bring them off those things which they have set up in that nature which is gone from the Light.

Now people are to be turned by the Light to Christ, their husband, the rock, the corner-stone, and are to be brought from their outward Crosses to the Cross of Christ, the power of God within them, and from the dead image to the image of God, which they have lost through their going-forth from the Light. And all these crosses of wood and stone, and the founder of them, must all be thrown down by the power of God, which is the Cross of Christ, and to the Light must they be turned, which answers to that of God in every one, before they come to feel Christ to rule and reign in them. Then the outward dead crosses of stone, wood, silver or gold they shall not need to have to put them in remembrance of Christ, or to bring him in to their minds, for such as are come to the Light feel Christ and his Cross, which is the power of God.

G. F. 1655

Friends,

Encourage not your wives nor children, in setting them up in the world's honour; for that which would do so in you is carnal, and the carnal mind is not subject to the law of God. If you do mind that which is of God in you, it will draw you up to God, out of the world's honour, and friendship, and words, and ways, and fellowships, and preferments, customs and fashions up to God's everlasting Kingdom, where is everlasting joy.

G. F. 1655

All Friends every where,

Dwell in the power of the Lord God, and live in it, for that brings all your souls into peace, into oneness, into God, from whence they come, who hath them all in his hand. And in the power ye will all come to feel the end of words, the life, from which all words of Truth were given forth; and all hasty, rash, loose, lustful spirits the power will strike down, for they beget nothing to God.

All spirits that are out of the Power must be judged with it, and kept subject, for that which lives in the Power is begotten by the Seed Christ, the New Man, that's made after God in righteousness and holiness. And none quench the Spirit's movings in the least degree, nor none go beyond. Nor none write, print, nor speak for God but as ye are moved of the Lord God, for that reacheth to that of God in others, and is effectual. And none stop writing or speaking, when ye are moved with the spirit of the Lord God, for the power of the Lord God is to order and to keep down that which would be hasty, or that which would not be obedient, for that leads into the wilderness, which the power and life, and Seed of God must be set a-top of, which keeps you over the world.

And all Friends every where, in all your Meetings know and feel the power and the Seed of the Lord God amongst you, over you and in you, and then ye will feel the presence of the Lord God dwelling in the midst of you. And to the Lord your hearts will be brought, and it will bring you nigh unto one another, and to come into sweet love and unity, and into easiness and openness of heart, and keep you over that which would stain you, or hurt you, or defile you. Whereby wisdom shall be given to you, with which ye shall be ordered to God's glory; whereby ye shall feel his blessing, and order the creatures to his praise.
This is to be read in all your Meetings

G. F. 1655

LETTER 53

Ep. 107

My dear Friends,

In the power of the everlasting God, which comprehends the power of darkness and all the temptations in it, dwell, which will keep and bring you to the word, which was in the beginning, which will keep you up to the life, and to feed upon the same, over the power of darkness. In that ye will find strength, and feel dominion and life, and that will let you see [that eternal time] before the Tempter was, and into that the Tempter cannot come, for the Power and Truth he is out of. And therefore let your faith be in the power, and over the weakness and temptations, and look not out at them, but look in the light and power of God at the Lord's strength, which will be made perfect in your weakest state. And look at the grace of God in all temptations, to bring your salvation; which is your teacher to teach you; for when ye do look or hearken to the temptations, ye go from your teacher, the grace of God, and so are darkened. The grace of God is sufficient in all temptations to lead out of them, and to keep over them.

G. F. 1655

A warning from the Lord for plainness of speech to be used. (To go among Friends)

Friends of God and Brethren,

This is a warning to you all from the Lord God and Jesus Christ, that all that ye speak, it may be in plainness of speech, and that it may proceed from that of God in you, that the light of Christ in all consciences, which he hath enlightened every one withal, may witness your words to be the words of life.

Therefore Friends, dwelling in the Light, it will bring you to plainness and few words, to live in the Life which gave forth the Scriptures, which was before the Scriptures were given forth; and with it ye may see their conditions, that dwelt in the Life and gave forth the scriptures.

And all who live in their own wills, and yet make a profession of the scriptures: there are the sects and opinions, and there is no unity, and they have not unity amongst themselves.

And all who are out of plainness, with the eternal Light, which Christ hath enlightened them withal, shall they be condemned and confounded in Time; for this Light was before Time, and is in Time, which lets every man and woman see their actions done in Time, and hating this Light, this is their condemnation.

If ye speak any thing contrary to the Light, with the Light ye are to be condemned. And if any among you do speak of former experiences, and not dwell in the Light, but in hypocrisy and presumption and envy, without the fear of God, ye are to be thrown down, and with the Light condemned. Therefore in the Light dwell and walk every one in particular; then ye will have unity with one another, and grow up to be trees of righteousness, the planting of the Lord.

G. F. 1656

LETTER 55 ·· Ep. 113

To a Friend in the Ministry, supposed E. B. [Edward Burrough]

Dear Brother,

Mind the Lord, and stand in his will and counsel. Look not forth at time nor place, but at thy Father's house, wheresoever thou art. And dwell in the pure measure of God in thee, and there thou wilt see the Lord God present with thee. For the bringing forth many out of prison, art thou there set: behold, the word of the Lord cannot be bound. The Lord God of Power give thee wisdom, courage, manhood and boldness to thresh down all deceit. Dear heart, be valiant, and mind the pure spirit of God in thee, to guide thee up unto God, to thunder down all deceit within and without. So farewell! God Almighty keep you all!

G. F. 1656

LETTER 56 ·· Ep. 116

Concerning Judging in Meetings

Friends,

Do not judge one another in Meetings, ye that do minister in the Meetings; for your so doing hath hurt the people, both within and without, and yourselves under their judgement ye have brought. And your judging one another in the Meetings hath emboldened others to quarrel, and judge you also in the Meetings. And this hath been out of all order, and the Church order also. Now, if ye have any thing to say to any, stay, till the Meeting be done, and then speak to them in private between yourselves, and do not lay open one another's weakness; for that is weakness and not wisdom to do so. For your judging one another in Meetings hath almost destroyed some Friends, and distracted them. And this is for want of love, that beareth all things, and therefore let it be amended. No more, but my love.

G. F. 1656

48

Friends,

If any amongst you have movings to do any service for the Lord, when they have done it, let them return again with speed to their habitation, and there serve the Lord in their generation, that no slothfulness may be amongst you. But keep all in diligence, that no occasion may be given to any to speak evil of the Truth, but that ye may answer that of God in all. So give no offence, for woe is to those by whom offences do come. Yet quench not the Spirit.

G. F. 1656

My dear Friends,

Keep your Meetings, and ye will feel the Seed to arise, though never a word be spoken amongst you. And be faithful, that ye may answer that of God in every one. And do not neglect your talent, but in the life and power of God live, which ye have received. And dear Friends, dwell in the life and power and love of God, and one towards another.

Friends, dwell in the measure of the spirit of God, and to it take heed, that in it ye may grow, for the true and lasting love proceeds from God, who is eternal. And abiding in the measure of Life, ye will have peace and love, that never changeth. If from the measure ye turn, iniquity gets up and the love waxeth cold, and in that lodge the evil thoughts, jealousies, evil will and murmurings. Wait in the Light, which is of God, that ye may all witness the Son of God, and witness that which shall never wither, so ye will see and feel God near.

G. F. 1656

This makes me want to cry - why can't our meeting be like this. How can we establish good order? How?

49

Friends,

Let no Friends go beyond their own measure given them of
God, nor rejoice in another man's line made ready to their
hands, lest that get up and would be justified, which is to be
condemned. And that which will boast and be justified in the
sight of man is out of the Kingdom excluded. Therefore in the
measure of Life wait, and with it be led to have power over your
own wills, (which are mortal and changeable), that the way of
righteousness may be found, where your wills are shut out,
which causes the hastiness and the strife to run into words without life, where judgement and condemnation doth overtake you.
Wherefore delight in judgement, which leads to the door of
mercy.

                                                     G. F. 1656

To Friends, to take care of such who suffer for owning the Truth

Friends,

In the wisdom and power of God dwell, by which all things
must be ordered to his glory, that with the wisdom of God ye
may order and preserve the creation, and everything that is
good.

And if any servants be convinced, and turned from their
places for Truth's sake, Friends be tender to them, that they be
not lost, but that they may be preserved. And if any soldiers be
put out of the army for Truth's sake, that they may be nourished
and cherished; or any children be turned from their parents, or
believing wives from their unbelieving husbands, that they may
be admonished to walk wisely towards them. And that all
prisoners, that have but little of their own, there may be care
taken for them, and for the lame and sick. And that, if any

Friends be oppressed any manner of way, others may take care to help them; that all may be as one family, building up one another, and helping one another. And if any desire Meetings any way for Truth's service, Friends not to look out but to dwell in the life and power of God, and therein to answer it.

And all Friends every where, in the power and life and Seed of God, keep all your Meetings, that over all the top-stone may be laid, and ye all as a sweet savour may be kept to God, and in the hearts of all people. And every one be obedient to the life and power of God, and that will keep you from being as a wilderness, but be faithful and still, till the winds cease, and the storm be over.

G. F. 1656

LETTER 61 ** Ep. 123

Men in the Fall are in the wars and strife, but Truth restores, and brings into peace

Dear Friends,

Mark, the Seed is not as the corn which grows upon the house-top that withers, for the leaves that this Seed brings forth never fade nor fall; for the leaves thereof heal the nations. The Second Adam goes over Adam in the Fall, and his quarrelling sons and daughters, who war with one another with their carnal weapons. But [those] who are in the noble and royal Seed are all in peace and in love, being in the Seed Christ, that never fell, nor ever will fall, nor never changed, nor never will change.

All that are in Adam in the Fall, both men and women, and there remaining in the Fall, they are never at rest nor peace, but are in travails, strife and fightings. For Adam in the Fall is all the (inward) foul weather; [his] whole family [are] in confusion, being gone from the spirit and witness of God in themselves, and the power and the Light; in which power, light, and spirit is the fellowship with God and one with another, through which they come out of Adam in the Fall into Second Adam the Quickener, who awakens Old Adam's children in the Fall out of their sleep of sin, and brings them out of his ways up to himself, the Way, Christ, that never fell nor changed, that never will leave the flock in cold weather, nor in the winter. For the Light, the Power and Truth, the Righteousness, did it ever leave you in any weather, or in any storms or tempests?

And so, his sheep know his voice and follow him, who gives them life abundantly, who saith to all that are dead in Adam, 'I am come that ye might have life'. Christ the second Adam is come that the dead in the First Adam might have life, and might be awakened to righteousness, who are asleep in the unrighteousness. And so, he doth invite all Adam's posterity to come to him, that all through him might believe, and come to life, and come up into peace and rest. Therefore all come out of Adam in the Fall, and haste to him that never fell, nor ever changed; in whom ye have both rest and peace, and life, that was with the Father before the world began.

And so, in the name of the Lord Jesus Christ, that never fell, keep your Meetings, ye who are gathered in his name; then ye will see over all the gatherings of Old Adam's sons and daughters. Ye being gathered into his name, Christ Jesus, feel the Seed set over all that makes to suffer; which was before that was, and will stand when that is all gone. So farewell.

G. F. 1656

Friends every where,

Dwell in the power of the Lord God, which is without end, in which ye may all have unity. And take heed of striving about earthly things, but that with the wisdom of God ye may come to be ordered, and order the creatures by that by which they were made.

And after that riches do increase, take heed of setting your hearts upon them, lest they become a curse and a plague to you. For when ye were faithful at the first, the world would refrain from you, and not have commerce with you; but after, when they saw ye were faithful and just in things, and righteous and honest in your tradings and dealings, then they came to have commerce and trade with you the more, because they know ye will not cheat them. Then ye came to have greater trading, double than ye ever had, and more than the world. But there is the danger and temptation to you, of drawing your minds into your business, and clogging them with it; so that ye can hardly do any thing to the service of God but there will be crying 'My business, my business'; and so therein ye do not come into the image of God. And so, when your minds are got into the riches, and cumbered therewith, ye go back into that ye were in before: and then, if the Lord God cross you, and stop you by sea and land, and take your goods and customers from you, that your minds should not be cumbered; then that mind that is cumbered, it will fret, being out of the power of God.

And all Friends, take heed of jars and strife, for that is it which will eat out the Seed in you. And therefore dwell in love and life, and in the power and Seed of God, which is the honourable, royal state.

In the time of the Law amongst the Jews there was fighting outwardly, but in the time of the gospel of Christ Jesus, who came to end the Law, they were to love enemies, and not kill them. But in the times since the days of the apostles, in the apostate-Christians' time, they are crying up the outward sword again. But who come to follow Christ, they are to reign in spirit over all these fighters with carnal weapons. Therefore those who are now come into the power of the Lord God, and to the Seed that is royal, keep your Meetings, that ye may come into [his power]; with which ye may (spiritually) reign over all the world, and rule in it over them and their vanities, and work them down without a carnal weapon.

And all Friends every where take heed of printing any thing more than ye are required of the Lord God.

And take heed of wandering up and down about needless occasions, for there is danger of getting into the careless words, out of seriousness and savouriness.

Take heed of slothfulness, and sleeping in your Meetings; for in so doing ye will be a bad example to others and hurt yourselves and them.

And take heed of going up and down to minister, but as ye are moved of the Lord God, or to speak in Meetings, or other places, for [it] is dangerous to lift them up, going among Meetings that are settled. For there is a difference betwixt Friends going into the world, and of coming amongst them that are come to silent Meetings, to feed there; for that which may be seasonable to the world may not be to them. Therefore let all live in the Seed, and wisdom and fear, and consider, before they utter that the Life be up, whereby all may be settled, and they themselves be washed. And dwell in the Seed, that ye all may know Christ come to reign in you. And in that ye will have unity in the record of life.

Let this be read in all your Meetings

G. F. 1656

Friends,

Let God's wisdom have the stay of your minds, and let it be the end of all your words. There is a day coming, wherein some may wish that they had walked in wisdom, as touching the weaknesses one of another, or the failings one of another; for what know ye who may stand or who may fall in the day of God's trial? Then many that have been unstable may wish that they had kept their secrets in their bosoms, and in God's wisdom sought to restore all and not to scatter, as that spirit doth which cannot bear and cover the weaknesses one of another. I have seen a great danger in this thing. Wherefore beware of that spirit which cannot bear one with another, or forgive one another, for that which cannot will bring a cloud over many, it may be in whole Meetings, for want of wisdom to be stayed in the meek Spirit, which tries all spirits, and gives clear sight of things.

Therefore I say, reach to the witness in all. So will ye stand for God, and God will bless you in the day of trial.

G. F. 1657

Friends,

Ye that are the prisoners of the Lord Jesus Christ in outward bonds, who witness him by whom the world was made, and who are his, ye are purchased with his blood, which washes and makes you clean, and justifies, whose bodies are his temple. Though he suffers you to be imprisoned, yet in his power your bodies are kept, and your spirits also, ye standing witnesses for your Master, for your King, for your prophet, for your covenant of Light, for your wisdom of God, for the Word and Power against the powers of darkness, who are out of the Light and Truth, who cannot bind, stop, nor limit the unlimited Power. And ye, who are the Lord's, are not your own. But they who are in their own time, see not the time which is in the Father's hand; their time is always, and they do their own works, and not the works of God, which the Son of God did.

G. F. 1657

Friends,

None owns the Light, as it is in Jesus, but he that owns the Light that Christ lighteth them withal. And none owns the Truth, but who owns the Light, that cometh from Christ the Truth; and none cometh to the Father, but such who owns the Light that cometh from Christ, which leads to him. Nor none owns the Son, except he owns the Light that cometh from him.

For dwelling in the Light that comes from Jesus, it leads out of wars, leads out of strife, leads out of the occasion of wars, and leads out of the earth up to God, and bringeth your minds to be in heaven.

G. F. 1657

All Friends every where, that do suffer for tithes, and are served with writs to answer at London, take copies of your subpoenas and writs, that ye may have them when ye appear, to show them to the court; whereby ye may be kept a-top of the persecutors and evil-doers. And keep a copy of all your sufferings for tithes in every county, that it may be laid on their heads that cause you to suffer.

And all Friends that suffer imprisonment, or are fined for not swearing, keep a copy of your sufferings in every county, and the men's names that cause you to suffer. And all Friends that suffer for not giving money for repairing of steeple-houses, keep copies of your sufferings in every county, and by whom. And as any are brought to suffer for these things or for not bowing to any deceit whatsoever, let a true and plain copy of such sufferings be sent up to London. And such as are moved of the Lord to go to steeple-houses, and are beat, knocked down, or imprisoned, let a copy of all such sufferings be sent up as aforesaid, that the things may be laid on the heads of them that caused the sufferings. And if any be beaten or wounded in going to Meetings, or struck or bruised in Meetings or taken out of Meetings and imprisoned, let copies of such things be taken, and sent as aforesaid, under the hands of two or three witnesses, that the Truth may be exalted, and the power and life of God lived in.

And if any Friends be summoned by writs, or subpoenaed to appear personally to answer for tithes, let them do it, that the Truth may stand over the head of the liar. And as ye are moved, be obedient to the Truth, that nothing may reign but the Truth. They say, 'Ye must appear personally', and when ye appear, say they do not mean so, but that ye must appear by an attorney. This is not the Truth; this is made up of a lie, and this is to be judged by them that dwell in the Truth.

If any Friends be moved to write to them who cause their sufferings, let them do it. Nevertheless let copies be sent of their sufferings as aforesaid. And also, any that suffer for not putting off their hats for conscience sake, let copies be sent up of these things likewise.

Let this be sent among all Friends in all counties in this nation

G. F. 1657

To Friends, to know one another in the Light

All Friends every where, meet together, and in the measure of God's spirit wait, that with it all your minds may be guided up to God, that ye may all come to know how ye may walk up to him in his wisdom, that it may be justified of you, and ye in it preserved up to God, and he glorified. And Friends, meet together, and know one another in that which is eternal, which was before the world was. For knowing one another only in the letter and the flesh differs you little from the beasts of the field, for what they know, they know naturally.

And if ye turn from this Light, ye grow strange, and so, neglecting Meetings, ye grow cold, and your minds run into the earth, and grow weary and slothful, and careless and heavy, and sottish, and dull and dead. Ye may speak then of things which were opened once from the Light, though now ye be turned from it; but with the Light, in which is the unity, all that is condemned. I charge you all in the presence of the living God that none boast yourselves above your measure of Light; if ye do ye will be buffeted. For with the Light man sees himself, which Light comes from Christ, who is the author and finisher of his faith; which faith gives him the victory over that which he sees to be contrary to the Light and the Word. And this is the one faith, and here the First Adam and the Second Adam are seen and known.

Let this be read among Friends every where

G. F. 1657

Friends,

There was a time when the apostles preached Christ, that died at Jerusalem, and they witnessed him forth, and brought for proof the prophets' testimonies. And they that preached Christ's sufferings at Jerusalem showed the fulfilling of the prophets and the law. And after[wards] the apostles preached Christ the substance, the end of all the types and figures, amongst them that had the prophets' words, and the law and the outward temple.

And then there was a time when the apostles preached *Christ in them* to them that did believe, and had received him. This was spoken to them that believed, who were the saints; to them *Christ in them* was preached, the substance of what the prophets prophesied of, and to believe in him, who was risen, the resurrection.

To the world the apostles preached repentance, and to believe in Jesus Christ, and taught faith towards God. But to them who were redeemed out of the world, in and to whom the Son of Man was made manifest, (who were brought to God, the judge of all, and to the church in God, and to the innumerable company of angels, and to the spirits of just men, who were made perfect in him through faith towards God), preaching repentance and the doctrine of baptism, was needless. He that can receive this, may, for there is no private meaning.

There is a time of preaching faith towards God, and there is a time to be brought to God. But such as are here, deny the first priesthood, and witness the second with the eternal spirit of God, a priest for ever, after the order of Melchisedech.

G. F. 1657

To Friends beyond sea, that have Blacks and Indian slaves

Dear Friends,

I was moved to write these things to you in all those plantations. God that made the world, and all things therein, and giveth life and breath to all, and they all have their life and moving, and their being in him; he is the God of the spirits of all flesh, and is no respecter of persons, but *whosoever feareth him, and worketh rightousness,* is accepted of him. And he hath made all nations of one blood to dwell upon the face of the earth, and his eyes are over all the works of his hands, and seeth everything that is done under the whole heavens; and the earth is the Lord's, and the fulness thereof. And he causeth the rain to fall upon the just and upon the unjust, and also he causeth the sun to shine upon the just and upon the unjust; and he commands to love all men, for Christ loved all, so that he died for sinners. And this is God's love to the world, in giving his Son into the world, that whosoever believeth in him should not perish. And he doth enlighten every man that cometh into the world, that they might believe in the Son. And the gospel is preached to every creature under heaven; which is the power that giveth liberty and freedom, and is glad tidings to every captivated creature under the whole heavens. And the word of God is in the heart and mouth to obey and do it, and not for them to ascend or descend for it; and this is the word of faith, which was and is preached. For Christ is given for a covenant to the people, and a light to the Gentiles, and to enlighten them; who is the glory of Israel, and God's salvation to the ends of the earth. And so ye are to have the mind of Christ, and to be merciful, as your heavenly Father is merciful.

G. F. 1657

Concerning the Light

Friends,

Ye that be turned to the Light, in it wait, in it meet together, that with it your hearts may be joined together up to Christ, the Head, from whence the Light doth come; with which ye may see all the world, and all the gatherings that are out of the Light. But ye, believing in the Light, and receiving it, ye receive and come into the covenant with God, and peace with God, and into that which gives the knowledge of his glory, and separates you from the world, and its image, and its fashion.

In the Light rejoicing and walking, ye receive the love of God shed abroad in your hearts; with that ye know the increase of God, and know God and his Law put in your minds, and in your hearts written, where the fear is placed, where the secrets of the Lord are revealed. Here is a joy in the Lord, where no flesh glories. In this waiting in the Light, the world where there is no end it gives you to see; and the power of the world which is to come ye will come to see, and be partakers of. Which power ye receiving, who are in the Light, it brings you to become the sons of God, and to be heirs of the world, where there is no end. Therefore, ye saints in the Light of the Most High God, walk worthy of the high calling! Keep your dominion, keep your place of rest in the power and strength of the Almighty, and meet together in the love, unity and peace, and know one another in this love, that changeth not.

G. F. 1657

Friends and Brethren every where,

Dwell in that which makes for peace and love; for blessed are the peace-makers, for theirs is the Kingdom that stands in righteousness, joy and peace in the Holy Ghost and in power. Therefore seek the peace, in which is the welfare and good of every one. And take heed of strife and contention, for that eats out the peace, for 'tis love that edifies the body. Therefore keep in the Seed, and know that which was afore enmity was, in which there's both peace and life.

And all be careful to watch over one another, for one another's good, and be patient, and keep low and down in the power of the Lord God. And take heed of any words or carriage that do not tend to building up in the love and life.

Therefore ye that have tasted of the power of God, and of his good word, and of his Light, wait for wisdom, and in it walk, that ye may be preserved in unity in the Light and Life, and in fellowship with God and one with another, that to the Lord God ye may be a good savour, and a blessing in your generation, strengthening one another in the faith, in the grace, in the word, by which all things were made. And keeping the word of patience, herein ye will see the Lord keeping you from all temptations. Live in that by which ye come to serve one another in love, Let not prejudice boil in any of your hearts, but let it be cast out by the power of God.

The grace of our Lord Jesus Christ be with you all, to teach, season, and establish you, which brings your salvation.

G. F. 1658

Friends,

Keep your Meetings in the power of God, and in his wisdom, and in the love of God, that by that ye may order all to his glory. And when Friends have finished their business, sit down and continue a while quietly, and wait upon the Lord, to feel him. And go not beyond the power, by which God Almighty may be felt among you. And so ye come to love Truth, and love Jesus Christ, and love holiness; and by the power ye come to love God, and praise him, and bless him, and magnify him, who lives for evermore. For the power of the Lord will work through all, if that ye follow it.

When ye do judge of matters, or when ye do judge of words, or when ye do judge of persons, all these are distinct things. A wise man will not give both his ears to one party, but reserve one for the other party, and will hear both, and then judge.

G. F. 1658

All Friends,

Be faithful in the power of God and his Seed, and mind the power of God, which was before the power of darkness and the Fall of Adam.

They have no more command to set up temples, tithes, oaths or swearing among the Christians since the apostles' days than the gentiles had to set up Diana's temple. For the temple worship, tithes and oaths Christ came to end, and to bring people out of them, and make them his temples, and to bring to *yea, yea,* and *nay, nay,* in their communications. And so before the Fall there were no oaths; in the Fall there were; but in the restoration there are to be no oaths, tithes, nor outward temples.

G. F. 1658

My dear Friends,

Be not carried away by good words and fair speeches, but every one have hold of the Truth in yourselves, by which ye may be stayed upon Christ, your bread of life.

Now Friends, who have denied the world's songs and singing, sing ye in the spirit, and with grace, making melody in your hearts to the Lord. And ye having denied the world's formal praying, pray ye always in the spirit, and watch in it. And ye having denied the world's giving of thanks, and their saying of grace and living out of it, do ye in every thing give thanks to the Lord through Jesus Christ. And ye, that have denied the world's praising God with their lips, whilst their hearts are afar off, do ye always praise the Lord night and day. And ye that have denied the world's fastings, and of their hanging down their heads like a bulrush for a day, who smite with the fist of wickedness, keep ye the fast of the Lord, that breaks the bond of iniquity and lets the oppressed go free; that your health may grow, and your Light may shine as the morning.

G. F. 1658

A General Epistle to them who are of the Royal Priesthood

Friends,

Let all that ye do, be done in the name of the Lord Jesus Christ. And all Friends, dwell in love, for that is the mark of a disciple; which love out of a pure heart is the end of the commandment, and fulfils the Law.

We need no Mass for to teach us, and we need not your Common Prayer, for the Spirit that gave forth the Scriptures teacheth us how to pray, sing, fast, and to give thanks; and how to honour and glorify God, and how to walk before him and men; and how to use all creatures upon earth.

We are a people that are redeemed from the earth and the world, and need none of your church-made faiths. The true faith changeth not, which is the gift of God, and a mystery held in a pure conscience, of which we are, and which is our faith.

Mass for the Papists, Common Prayer for the Episcopal men, and the Directory for the Presbyterians; Church-made and framed faith for the Independents and Mixed Baptists [and others]. [They] have had their fellowships, for which they fought, and about which carnal weapons got up, since the days of the apostles, but the fellowship of the Spirit remains, which hath spiritual weapons. And men stand in doubts and questions, and have no assurance in their religion, but that of God stands in them all bound. Our faith, our church, our unity is in the Spirit, and our Word at which we tremble was in the beginning before your Church-made faiths, and our unity, church, and fellowship will stand when they are all ended.

'Forgive us, as we forgive them', cry Papists, cry Episcopals, [and the rest]. These cry the Lord's Prayer, and then like a company of senseless men fall a-fighting with one another about their trespasses and debts, and never mind what they prayed, as though they never looked for forgiveness, and to receive the things they prayed for, that fall a-persecuting and imprisoning one another, and taking their brethren and fellow-servants by the throat about religion, [who] in their prayers said 'Father, forgive us, as we forgive them', and will not forgive.

And so, Friends, dwell in the Seed of God, which is the heir of the power of the world without end. In that keep your Meetings.

G. F. 1659

LETTER 76 ·   Ep. 173

All Friends,

Take heed of running on in a form, lest ye do lose the Power. But keep in the Power and Seed of God. And at any disputes take heed. And if babblers come, and janglers say, they have a bad Meeting, the murmuring nature getteth up, out of patience, and [out of] the Seed, which beareth and suffereth all things, which keepeth down all that which causeth lifting up, murmuring and disputing. That which keeps down that which doth change is the peace and the corner-stone, and the stayedness in the Seed and the Life.

G. F. 1659

LETTER 77 ·   *of 108*   Ep. 177

All Friends every where, who are dead to all carnal weapons, and have beaten them to pieces, stand in that which takes away the occasion of wars, in the Power which saves men's lives, and destroys none, nor would have others. And as for the rulers, that are to keep peace, for peace's sake and the advantage of Truth, give them their tribute. But to bear and carry carnal weapons to fight with, the men of peace cannot act in such things, but have paid their tribute. Which they may still do for peace sake, and not hold back the earth, but go over it; and in so doing, Friends may better claim their liberty.

G. F. 1659

66

To Friends in Barbadoes, Virginia, New England and all the islands about

Friends and Brethren, who are made partakers of the power of the world that is without end, in that feel one another, and know one another, and in the Life, that the top-stone may be laid over all, and ye all in the wisdom, life and Seed in your measures may be preserved, spreading the Truth abroad, confounding the deceit, and answering the witness of God in all, (to which they must be brought, before their minds can be turned to God). For all Christendom, which hath gotten the word of the prophets, Christ and the apostles, that are not in the spirit and power as they were in that gave them forth, are all in heaps about them, and not in unity, being out of the Spirit.

And my dear Friends, be faithful and quench not the Spirit, but be obedient to the Truth, and spread it abroad, which must go over all the world, to professors, Jews, Christians, and heathen, to the answering the witness of God in them all, that they may come to the Truth, which answers the witness in them, to be made free by it.

G. F. 1659

Friends,

Live in the unchangeable power of God, which will keep you in righteousness and truth and love and unity and dominion over all the unclean spirits and rough ways and mountains within and without. And none abuse it, but all patiently in the power of the Lord wait, that with it ye may all be kept low, in love and unity with God, and one with another; that in the Seed ye may be kept.

And all be diligent in your places serving the Lord, and that your spirits may not be plucked down with earthly things, nor limited by them; but that in the power of the Lord God ye may act over them out of the entanglements and thraldom of them, and out of the vain inventions of men, but keep in the power of the Lord God over them. For that is it which will keep you out of the changeable things, and there the Seed comes up. Therefore feel it in the heart which is more than the head or the tongue.

Therefore all be wise in the wisdom of God, and let every one's eye be unto that wisdom, which the departing from sin and evil is the beginning of, that with it ye may be ordered and do whatsoever ye have to do. In that ye will feel his presence and blessing. And your growth in the Seed is in the silence, where ye may all feel a feeding of the bread of life. And all Friends, keep in the wisdom of the Lord, that is pure and holy from above. And there innocency and simplicity and nakedness of heart and spirit is lived in.

G. F. 1659

P.S. If any Friends have friends (or relations) beyond sea, send them books or papers, and be diligent to spread the Truth. And send Latin books, or French books, or other books, to Leghorn, France, Poland, Norway, Low Countries &c.

Friends,

Dwell in patience and in peace and love and unity one with another. And be subject in the power, and life and wisdom of God, to God and in one another, that in it ye may be as a pleasant field to the Lord God, and as the lilies and the flowers and the buds feeling the pleasant showers, and the streams of life from the living God flowing into you, whereby the presence and blessing of the Lord God Almighty amongst you all may be felt.

G. F. 1659

LETTER 81 •   Ep. 189

To Friends in New England and Virginia

My dear Friends,

Be faithful to the Lord in the Truth, and in his power and wisdom be valiant for it upon the earth, and spread it abroad, and confound deceit. To all nations of mankind the everlasting Gospel, the power of God, is to be preached, through which life and immortality shall come to light; in which Power is the fellowship. Therefore this is the word of the Lord to you all; those that are convinced by the power of the Lord God and the Light, let them dwell in it, in which they may have unity. For the Lord hath a Seed that ways, if ye in patience all of you wait, and not matter the weather, the storms, the winds, the hail, the rain, when ye are to sow the seed, nor the rough ground that is to be tilled. For the husbandman waits patiently after the seed is sown. There is a winter before the summer comes. And there must be a great work before the misty heathen be cleared in their understandings (that are so naturally) and the dark air be driven back, and the Prince of life and Light be witnessed.

Ye may write over, how things are there; for Truth is well here, and spreads abroad in the world in other nations, and is of a good report

G. F.

Reading, the 15th of the 8th Month, 1659.

LETTER 82 '   Ep. 198

Dear Friends,

Keep over all that which tends to strife, in the Seed Christ, in which is peace and life, for that which tends to strife and yet is in a feigned flattery, will corrupt you. And therefore live in that which is pure and steadfast, and in that know one another.

And lay hands on no man suddenly, for that which is fickle and changeable will bring people into an unsettled state, and keep them out of their own conditions, and bring into a questioning state. And therefore keep in the Seed, and Light and power of Christ, in which ye may walk safely, and not give away your power. And in it keep your Meetings, and be quiet, and live.

And be faithful, that the Seed Christ may reign in you, and among you. For the Truth is over all and reigns. And so be valiant for it upon the earth.

G. F.

Lancaster Prison, the 2nd of the 5th Month, 1660.

The line of righteousness and judgement stretched forth over all merchants &c.

All Friends every where,

Live in the Seed of God, which is the righteousness itself, and inherits the wisdom, and is the wisdom itself. With which wisdom ye may order, rule and govern all things which are under your hands (which God hath given you) to his glory. Govern and order with his wisdom all the creatures that ye have under you, and all exchangings, merchandising, husbandry.

So, this is the word of the Lord God to you all. Do rightly, whether ye be tradesmen, of what calling or profession or sort so ever, or husbandmen. Do rightly, justly, truly, holily, equally to all people in all things; and that is according to that of God in every man, and the witness of God, and the wisdom of God, and the life of God in yourselves; and there ye are serviceable in your generation, labouring in the thing that is good, which does not spoil, nor destroy, nor waste the creation upon the lusts.

And all merchants and seamen: Wrong no man, overreach no man (if it may be never so much to your advantage). Live in the life of Truth, and let the Truth speak in all things, and righteousness, and let justice be acted, and holiness in all things, without any guile, fraud, or deceit.

All husbandmen and dealers about husbandry: do justly, whether ye be masters or servants, fathers or mothers, sons or daughters, to one another and to all; in that ye will have peace and see God. Wrong no man, nor covet nor cheat, nor oppress, nor defraud any man in any case, but keep your dominion in the Truth.

So that is the word of God to you all Friends, of whatsoever calling ye be: live in the power of Truth, and wisdom of God, to answer that just principle of God in all people upon the earth. So, let your lives preach, let your light shine, that your works may be seen, that your Father may be glorified. This hath the praise of God, and they who do so come to answer that which God requires, to love mercy, do justly, and to walk humbly with God.

And all, of what trade or calling soever: keep out of debts. Owe no man anything but love. Go not beyond your estates, lest ye bring yourselves to trouble, and cumber, and snare. For a man that would be great, and goes beyond his estate, lifts himself up, runs into debt, and lives highly of other men's means; he is a waster of other men's, and a destroyer. He is not serviceable to the creation, but a destroyer of the creation and creatures.

And all Friends that are shopkeepers or merchants, do not go beyond your capacity, nor reach after things more than ye can justly perform, and answer all men, that ye may not break your words and promises. And none to be negligent in their business, but give an account by words or writing how things are with them, when others write to them, so that none may wrong one another in these outward things, nor oppress one another, but be serviceable to one another.

So every one strive to be rich in the life, and the things of the Kingdom that hath no end; for he that covets to be rich in the things of this world, falls into many snares and hurtful lusts. And therefore let him that buys, or sells, or possesses, or uses this world, be as if he did not. Let them be masters over the world in the power and spirit of God, and let them know that they owe no man anything but love; yet serve God in Truth, and one another in their generation.

For, Friends, if ye be not faithful in the outward treasure, and outward Mammon, who will trust you with the true Treasure? Or who can believe that ye have the true Treasure, but that ye speak by hearsay of it?

So all ye, that know his Power and Spirit, live in it, that ye may glorify God in all your lives, and conversations, and words, that ye may answer that of God in all; that ye may glorify God in your bodies, souls and spirits, which are his, who hath made them, and gives them to you for that end. So the Lord God

Almighty keep and preserve you faithful in all things to his glory and honour for ever!

G. F. 1661

In the power of God that is everlasting, and doth remain in this your day of trial, in it stand, of which ye are partakers, and in it is your peace and kingdom. And though ye have not a foot of ground to stand upon, yet ye have the power of God to skip and leap in; [if ye are] standing in that which is your life, that is everlasting. Who by the power of God are gathered up to the beginning, to the endless life, who have your Meetings in it, neither death, nor the power of it, can separate you from the power of God, for it was before death. In that are your living Meetings and joinings, and the building up of the spiritual households of living stones, gathered by and through the power of God.

Stand fast therefore in your confidence in the power of God and Light, which rules over powers, thrones, principalities and dominions. The power of God goes over them, and ye living in it, nothing can separate you from the love of God, which ye have in Christ the Seed, which was before the world began, glorified with the Father. And prisons, fetters, dungeons, and sufferings, what are they to you, who are married to the Lamb who was slain from the foundation of the world? Whom neither death, grave, nor all the powers of the world were able to contain; but over all he rose (the Seed) and reigns. And ye that partake of the Power have power with God. In that we need not bid you: keep your Meetings. Be at peace with one another, and in love and tenderness, and in the wisdom of God, order and preserve and nourish all things to his glory.

G. F. 1661

Dear Friends,

All ye prisoners of the Lord for his Truth sake, and for keeping the testimony of Jesus Christ against all the inventions, traditions, will-worships, feigned humilities and self-righteousnesses that are in the Fall, who have no weapons but carnal, like themselves; your patience must overcome all the rough spirits in the world, and your love must bear all things. So be meek and low, and then ye follow the example of Christ, and come to bear the image of the Just, who suffered by the unjust; and put on his righteousness, who suffered by the unrighteous, whose back was struck, hair plucked off, and face was spit upon, and yet cried, 'Father, forgive them'. Here he kept his dominion, though a sufferer, which the followers of the Lamb do in measure attain to.

And all Friends, your sufferings ye may gently send to them, which make you to suffer, whether it be Sheriffs, Deputy-Lieutenants, or Justices, and let them see Christ's mind nor the disciples' were not to imprison any, nor did they imprison any; whereby ye may clear your innocency to the consciences and witnesses of God in all men.

G. F. 1661

Friends,

The deceivers are not worth the setting foot after; and yet ask them for what end Christ came. They will say 'To destroy the Devil and his works'. And then ask them if the body of sin and death be not the Devil's work and imperfection. They will say 'yes'. And so are in confusion. Christ came to destroy the Devil and his works, they say, and yet they must carry them to the grave. People are saved by Christ, they say, but while you are upon earth you must not be made free from sin. This is as much as if one should be in Turkey a slave, chained to a boat, and one should come to redeem him to go into his own country; but say the Turks, 'Thou art redeemed, but whilst thou art upon the earth thou must not go out of Turkey, nor have the chain off thee'. So you are redeemed, but must carry a body of sin and death about you and cannot go to your father Adam's house before he fell, but you must live in your father Adam's house in the Fall while ye be upon the earth!

But, I say, you are redeemed by Christ. It cost him his blood to purchase man out of this state he is in, in the Fall, and bring him up to the state man was in before he fell; so Christ became a curse to bring man out of the curse, and bore the wrath to bring man to the peace of God, that he might come to the blessed state, and to Adam's state he was in before he fell; and not only thither, but to a state in Christ that shall never fall. And this is my testimony to you, and to all people upon the earth.

G. F. 1662

Dear Friends,

Sing and rejoice, ye children of the Day, and of the Light; for the Lord is at work in this thick night of darkness that may be felt. And Truth doth flourish as the rose, and the lilies do grow among the thorns, and the plants a-top of the hills, and upon them the lambs do skip and play. And never heed the tempests nor the storms, floods nor rains, for the Seed Christ is over all, and doth reign. And so, be of good faith and valiant for the Truth; for the Truth can live in the gaols. And fear not the loss of the fleece for it will grow again; and follow the Lamb, if it be under the beast's horns, or under the beast's heels, for the Lamb shall have victory over them all.

And so all live in the Seed Christ, your Way that never fell; and you do see over all the ways of Adam's and Eve's sons and daughters in the Fall. And in the Seed Christ your Way, you have life and peace; and there you do see over all the ways of Adam in the Fall, in which there is no peace. So in the Seed Christ stand and dwell.

G. F.

The 9th Month, 1663.

Friends,

And now Friends, here you may discern what is set up by
Christ and his spirit, and what is set up by man. For Christ who
ended the Jews' law and commandment, who preached and
taught his disciples, who were to go into all nations to preach the
gospel, to gather people unto him, and to establish Churches, he
gave forth no command nor order that they that would not hear
them nor receive them, should be persecuted, imprisoned, or
banished, though he suffered, and was blasphemed and
persecuted, and his apostles, for publishing forth the Truth. He
rebuked them that would have had men's lives destroyed, and
said he came to save men's lives. And the apostles, and the true
Church in the primitive times, before the apostacy, that were in
the spirit of Christ Jesus, walked in the doctrine of Christ and
his commands, and did not persecute any about religion, and if
[any] did reject the Church's counsel, they were to be left as
heathen, which was the utmost penalty. And here you may see
the spirit of Christ did not persecute any for not observing that
which it gave forth and set up, which it received from God.

G. F. 1664

The saints' weapons are spiritual, that the blessing of God may come upon all men

Friends,

We are not against any man, but desire that the blessing of the Lord may come upon all men, and that which brings the curse may be destroyed; and in patience do we wait for that, and with spiritual weapons do we wrestle, and not against any man's or woman's person; for amongst us Christ is King. And whoever dwells in righteousness, (man or woman), and loves mercy, and doth justly, and walks humbly with God, and hath the humility which goes before the honour, we are not against. But whosoever doth unrighteously, and will have honour before humility, God will overturn such by his power. And in that let your faith be, for we look not at persons, but at the power of God, and know the reign of Christ amongst us. And, as it is said, 'God save the King' or 'God bless the King', we would not have him nor any man destroyed, but saved, and so blessed.

And the saved man will not suffer anything to rule that destroys, and so our mind is that we would that all men were saved, and come to the knowledge of the Truth, which the persecutors are out of.

G. F. 1666

Friends,

Keep your Meetings in the power of the Lord God, that hath gathered you; and none quench the Spirit, nor despise prophesying, but keep up your testimony in public and in private.

Concerning the Women's Meetings: encourage all the women of families, that are convinced and mind virtue, and love Truth and walk in it, that they may come up into God's service, that they may be serviceable in their generation and come into the practice of the pure religion, that every one may come to know their duty in it, and their service in the power and wisdom of God. For people must not always be talking and hearing, but they must come into obedience to the great God of heaven and earth.

And so, that none may stand idle out of the vineyard, and out of the service, and out of their duty, (for such will talk and tattle and judge with evil thoughts what they in the vineyard say and do), the power of the Lord God calls all into their duty and service. For all that are out of this, though they may have the knowledge of it, yet are not serviceable in the creation, nor in their generation.

And therefore train up your young women to know their duty in this thing; for all Truth's business you are to do in the power and wisdom of God, by which you are kept open to the Lord, to receive of his gifts and graces, through which you are to minister one to another. And all keeping in his Life, there is none to stop its flowings, but through it you are all watered, as a garden of plants. And so, be faithful and diligent.

And make all the sober women, both of town and country, acquainted with this thing. And read this in your Monthly Meetings.

So, no more but my love.

G. F. 1666

LETTER 91[•]   Ep. 250

Friends,

Keep out of the vain fashions of the world; let not your eyes and minds and spirits run after every fashion in apparel of the nations; for that will lead you from the solid life. But mind that which is sober and modest, and so keep to your plain fashions. And Friends that see that world so often alter their fashions, if you follow them, in that ye cannot judge the world, but the world will rather judge you. Therefore take heed of the world's fashions, lest ye be moulded up into their spirit, and that will bring you to slight Truth, and through such foolish toys and fading things you may lose your conditions. Therefore take heed of the world's vanity, and trust not in uncertain riches, neither covet the riches of this world, but mind the hidden man of the heart, which is a meek and quiet spirit.

And keep to justice and truth in all your dealings and tradings, that your lives and conversations may preach to all that you have to deal withal.

G. F. 1667

LETTER 92 •   Ep. 251

My dear Friends in the Truth and Seed of God,

Let purity and Life flow from the head to the feet, that righteousness and judgement may flow down our streets as a stream. For you know that formerly we did cry against the powers of the earth because that judgement, and justice, and righteousness did not flow down their streets. And now that Friends are become a great people shall not judgement and justice and righteousness flow down our streets as a stream and a flood, to drive away all the filth from amongst us?

And now that Friends are become a good savour in the hearts of all people, and God having given them his dominion and favour, lose it not, but rather increase it in the Life. For at first ye know that many could not take so much money in your trade as to buy bread with. All people stood aloof of you when you stood upright and gave them the plain language and were at a word; but now you, through the Life, come to answer that of God in all, they say they will trust you before their own people, knowing that you will not cheat, nor wrong, nor oppress them. For the cry is now, among those that are without, 'Where is there a Quaker of such and such a trade?' So that they will deal with Friends before they will deal with their own.

Oh, therefore Friends, who have purchased this through great sufferings, lose not this great favour which God hath given unto you, but that you may answer the witness of God in every man, which witnesseth to your faithfulness, that they may glorify your Father on your behalf.

And now, Friends, if there be any oppression or defrauding, through the freedom which God hath given you, the world will see such, and say 'The Quakers are not as they were'. Therefore such should be exhorted to equity and truth. And therefore Friends, all uncleanness, and unfaithfulness, and youthful ways of running out and lifting up must be exhorted and reproved, that truth and righteousness may flow, through which you may keep that which you have bought and kept through great sufferings, and some to death; that Truth in all things may be adorned.

Let this be read in all your men and women's Meetings, who are to take notice of all such things. So, no more but my love in the universal Seed of God.

G. F. 1667

To Friends in Holland

Dear Friends,

In the everlasting power of the Lord God I salute all the faithful and upright, amongst whom the Lord hath joy and delight.

And so, Friends, all sufferings of Friends for conscience sake to Christ, in Holland, in Germany, in Zealand, in Gilderland, in the Palatinate, in Freezland, Sweedland, Switzerland, and Hambrough, send an account for what they have suffered, and by whom; together with the examples that are fallen upon their persecutors, with their mittimusses and examinations; send all these to London, to Friends there; that if any ambassadors or agents out of any of those places come to London Friends may make application to them; for there are some Friends who are ordered to take knowledge of such things.

And likewise, if any Friends have come over into those parts of the world, and have not walked answerable to the gospel of Truth, whether they have been such who have come over to minister, or seamen, or factors, or merchants, or masters of ships, whereby the Lord hath been dishonoured. And also all such who have not been faithful in their callings between man and man, and have been exactors, and have not been true to their word. That a list of all such may be gathered up, and sent over to London to such who are to receive them; and if they condemn those things and have given forth a paper of condemnation against them, that we may have a copy of it also, to take away the reproach of their transgressions from Friends.

And let the faithful Friends amongst you meet together, to consider and take care about these things.

G. F. 1667

All Friends and people,

No man after he hath beaten his child, hateth him ever afterwards, but loveth him, if he repent and amends; so doth the eternal Father. And if the child be fallen down into the dirt, he doth not go and tumble him more into the dirt, or into the ditch, and there let him lie in the dirt and ditch, but takes him out and washes him; and so doth the heavenly Father, which leads his children by his hand, and dandles them upon his knee. And so, all that be called fathers in the Truth, or mothers, their tenderness should be the same to all little children in the Truth, that can hardly go without leading, that sometimes may fall into the dirt and ditch, and slip aside, and then be troubled and cry. To such there should be tenderness shown, to wash them, and help them. And love to such should be manifest; for there is a difference between a stubborn, rebellious and wilful child, and one that is penitent; for those must have great chastisements and stripes, that knows the will of their Father and does it not.

Christ makes an end of sin, and brings in everlasting righteousness into them. But first he condemns the sin that is in their flesh, all sin, whatsoever it is.

They that are led by the spirit of God are the sons of God; and all they that quench the spirit of God, and hate the Light of Christ, sure you may all see such are not the sons of God and do not the works of God, though they may profess the Scriptures from the beginning of *Genesis* to the end of *Revelation*.

The true fellowship hath been lost, and sanctification, and belief, and the righteousness, since the apostles' days; for many have had the letter, but lost the Life; the notion, but lost the possession; the profession, but lost the substance, Christ Jesus. Every one that cometh into the world are enlightened by Christ, that they should believe in the Light, as he commands them, and so become children of the Light; and he that believes, overcomes the world. And if there be no overcoming on this side of the grave, as the world's preachers say, then there is no true believing on this side of the grave, and therefore the world is not overcome in them. This belief in Christ, which passes from death to life, it takes away the root of sin.

So from this sanctifying belief you are all erred from the apostles' days, but have made beliefs and creeds of your own, and then say there is no overcoming on this side of the grave. You may as well say, there is no true belief.

G. F. 1668

LETTER 95 ·   Ep. 264

Friends,

Fellowship must be in the spirit, and all Friends must know one another in the spirit and power of God. And Friends, my desire is that ye may all be preserved in the Lord's power, and in his everlasting Seed, and so in the order of the gospel, and in the government of Christ Jesus, of the increase of which there is no end. Now all Friends, who have known the power of God, and do believe in the Light of Christ, who is your high-priest, you come to know him to be your teacher, and to hear him in all things, that God may work all your works in you and for you.

Now concerning gospel-order; though the doctrine of Jesus Christ requireth his people to admonish a brother or sister twice, before they tell the Church, yet that limiteth none, but that they not less than twice admonish their brother or sister. And it is desired of all that before they publicly complain, they wait in the power of God to feel if there is no more required of them to their brother or sister, before they expose him or her to the Church. And all such as behold their brother or sister in a transgression, go not in a rough light or upbraiding way to him or her, but in the power of the Lord, and spirit of the Lamb, and in the wisdom and love of the Truth, which suffers thereby, to admonish such an offender. So may the soul of a brother or sister be seasonably and effectually reached unto and over-come, and they may have cause to bless the name of the Lord on their behalf.

And be it known unto all, we cast out none from among us; for if they go from the Light and the Spirit, in which our unity is, they cast out themselves. And it has been our way to admonish them, that they may come to that spirit and light of God which they are gone from, and so come into the unity again. For our fellowship stands in the Light, and if they will not hear our admonitions, the Light condemns them, and then goes out the testimony of Truth against them.

And dear Friends, dwell in the everlasting power of God, that his wisdom you may receive, which is pure and gentle from above, by which all things were made; by which wisdom you may order all things to the glory of God. The poor, the sick, the widows, the fatherless, the prisoners be tender of, and feel every one's condition, as your own, and let nothing be lacking amongst you, according to the apostle's doctrine to the Church of God in old time; and if nothing be lacking, all is well. And the least member in the Church hath an office, and is serviceable; and every member hath need one of another.

And dear Friends, do all that you do in peace and love, and in the fear of God, condescending one unto another, in the simplicity and innocency of Life and Truth, and in the wisdom of God, that that may be every one's crown, that nothing may be done in strife, for you are called to peace and holiness, in which the Kingdom stands, and to serve one another in love.

G. F. 1669

To ministering Friends

Friends,

Every one that feels the Power stirring in them to minister, when they have done, let them live in the Power, in the Truth and in the Grace, that keeps in the seasoned words, and in a stablished and seasoned life. And so all may minister as they have received the Grace. For the true labourers in the vineyard do answer that of God; the true ministers bring people to that which is to instruct them, viz, the spirit of God. They answer the Spirit, and the Grace and Truth in all.

G. F. 1669

To Friends in Ireland

Keep to the equal measure and weight in all things, both inwardly and outwardly, that you may answer equity, answer Truth in the oppressed, and the Spirit, and Grace, and Light in all people. And so, being kept in righteousness, and equity, and truth, and holiness, that preserves you over the inequality, injustice, and the false measure and weight, and balance in all things, both inward and outward. And this keeps your eye open, keeps you in a feeling sense, keeps you in understanding and true wisdom, and true knowledge, what you are to answer all men in righteousness, truth and equity, both inward and outward.

And this is to all you that have purchased any Irish land, to answer that which is true, and just and even and equal in yourselves and every man and woman; that you may be preserved in the sense and favour of God, to answer the good and righteous principle in all, by which they may know the just and true God in all his works and outgoings.

G. F. 1669

To Friends at Bristol in time of suffering

Dear Friends,

Now is the time for you to stand; therefore put on the whole armour of God, from the crown of the head unto the soles of your feet, that you may stand in the possession of Life. And you that have been public men, and formerly did travel abroad, mind to keep up your testimony, both in the city and the countries, that you may encourage Friends to keep up their Meetings as usual there-away; so that none faint in the time of trial, but that all may be encouraged, both small and great, to stand faithful to the Lord God, and his power and truth; that their heads may not sink in the storms, but be kept above the waves.

So, go into your Meeting Houses as at other times. And keep up your public testimony, and visit Friends thereabouts, now in this time of storm; for there is your crown, in the universal power and spirit of God. So let your minds and souls, and hearts be kept above all outward and visible things. Few travel now in the countries: it may be well to visit them, lest any should faint. Stir up one another in that which is good, and to faithfulness in the Truth this day. And let your minds be kept above all visible things; for God took care for man in the beginning, and set him above the works of his hands. And therefore mind the heavenly Treasure, that will never fade away, and dwell in the Seed, in which you may know your election.

It's hard for me to give forth in writing what is before me, because of my bodily weakness, but I was desirous in some measure to ease my mind, desiring that you may stand fast, and faithful to Truth. Of my travels and weakness it's like you have heard, and of my afflictions, both by them that are without, and also by them that are within, which is hard to be uttered and spoken. *My love to all faithful Friends.*

G. F.

The 2nd of the 11th Month, 1670.

Dear Friends and Brethren,

See that all live in the peaceable and blessed Truth, into which no enmity can come; for the blessed Seed, Christ Jesus, takes away the curse; [in] the increase of whose government there is no end; who rules in righteousness amongst the righteous for ever. And see this righteousness, in which you all have peace, run down and flow as a stream among you, who are begotten again into a lively hope, and born again by the Immortal Seed of the Word of God. And you who have received Christ have received power to become the sons of God, and to believe in the Light, in obedience to Christ's command, by which you become children of the Light, and children of the Day. Therefore this I say unto you: let no man abuse this power; [but] keep the gospel-order, which was before any impurity was, and will be when it is gone. So that in all your Men and Women's Meetings see that virtue flow, and see that all your words be gracious, and see that love flow, which bears all things, that kindness, tenderness and gentleness may be among you, and that the fruits of the good spirit may abound; for nothing that is unclean must enter into God's kingdom, which stands in righteousness, and in holiness.

And see in all your Men and Women's Meetings that God be no ways dishonoured, nor the pure and blessed name of Christ, in which you are gathered, be blasphemed; but that in all things God may be glorified, exalted and honoured; for you have the Light to see all evil, and the Power to withstand it, and to see that nothing be lacking; then all will be well among you; for God is rich, and abundance of his riches ye have received. And so this is a warning and a charge to you all, in the presence of the living God, that you keep up the testimony of Jesus, against all that which is contrary to Jesus the heavenly man, that your fruits may appear to his glory, and your works to his praise.

And so the power of God preserve you all, and keep you in his blessed Seed, Christ Jesus, that none of you may be without a minister, without a priest, or without a prophet, or without a shepherd, or without a bishop, but let every one receive him in his offices. Then you all have One, who will exercise his offices in you all, whom God hath given for a leader and a covenant; yea, an everlasting leader, who was the foundation of the prophets and apostles, and is to us this day.

And so be valiant for the Truth upon the earth, in the Seed, Christ Jesus, that through him who destroys death you may have a crown of life, and through him you may be one another's crown and joy in the Lord.

G. F. 1671

P.S. I am just now upon leaving this island, where I have had very great and blessed service, though I underwent very great weights and travels, but all is well.

LETTER 100 ·   Ep. 287

Friends,

Consider, you that have known the mercies of the Lord God, and of Jesus Christ, look back and see how they that had known much of God, how soon they forgot him, as in the days of the old world, and in the days of Moses, and in the days of the Judges, how they soon forgot God, that had done great things for them, and forsook God and his way, and religion, and worship, and followed such gods as men had made. And in the days of the Prophets, [see] how the people forsook the Lord God, and [how] in the days of Christ and his apostles they were mostly gone astray from God, though they kept an outward profession of their words, yet denied Christ in his Light, and Life, and Power, who was the end of the Law and the Prophets.

And [of] them that did receive Christ Jesus, and believed in him, in a few ages after the apostles [see] how most of

Christendom ran from the Life into death, and ran from the Light into darkness, and from the worship in the Spirit and the Truth, that Christ had set up, and went from the true Church; and from Christ, the way to God, after the ways that men had made; and from the religion that is pure from above, after the religions that men have made. And so now, the gospel is preached again; and the living way (Christ), and his religion and worship is set up and received of many, and they come to the true worship, which is of God.

And all be faithful, and take heed of running back again where you were before, lest you and your children perish, as others have done, that forsook the Lord God of mercies. And therefore train up your children in the fear of God, and in the way of Christ, and in his worship and religion, that they may observe and keep in it when you are gone.

And walk in the Spirit and Truth, in which God is worshipped, and keep in the order of the gospel that nothing may get betwixt you and God. And be obedient to the Law that God hath written in your hearts, and put into your minds, that you may be the children of the new covenant; and that you may be the royal priesthood, offering up to God the spiritual sacrifices. And sitting under your teacher, the grace of God, which bringeth salvation, seasoneth your words, and establisheth your hearts. And this grace is sufficient.

G. F. 1671

To Friends in New-England, Virginia and Barbadoes

Dear Friends,

Be faithful in the power of the Lord God, in what you know, and then the Lord will preserve you; that you may answer the witness of God in every man, whether they are the heathen, that do not profess Christ, or whether they are such as do profess Christ, that have the form of godliness and be out of the Power.

And keep your Meetings, ye that know the Power of the Lord and feel it, that in it you may have unity with God, and one with another.

Therefore keep your Meetings, and dwell in the Power of Truth, and know it in one another, and be one in the Light, that you may be kept in peace and love, in the power of God, that you may know the mystery of the gospel. And all that ever you do, do in love; do nothing in strife, but in love that edifies the body of Christ, which is the Church.

So as any is moved to go amongst the heathen, in the power and love of God, to preach the gospel, (which is the love of God to them), to bring them to the power of God; to that God, which is the God of the stones, which they make idols of, and the God of the trees, earth, brass, iron and gold, which they make gods of, for those are dead gods that are made with men's hands.

He is the living God that clothes the earth with grass and herbs, and causes the trees to grow and bring forth food for you; and makes the fishes of the sea to breathe and live, and makes the fowls of the air to breed, and causes the roe and the hind, and all the creatures, and all the beasts of the earth to bring forth, whereby they may be food for you.

He is the living God, and causes the stars to arise in the night, to give you light; and the moon to arise to be a light in the night. He is the living God that causes the sun to give warmth unto you, to nourish you when you are cold. He is the living God, that causes the snow and frost to melt, and causes the rain to water the plants. He is the living God, that made the heaven and the earth, and the clouds, and causes the springs to break out of the rocks; and divided the great sea from the earth, and divided the light from the darkness, by which it's called day, and the darkness night; and divided the great waters from the earth, and gathered them together: which great waters he called sea, and the dry land earth. He is to be worshipped that doth this.

He is the living God that gives you breath and life and strength, and gives you the beasts and the cattle, whereby you may be fed and clothed. He is the living God and he is to be worshipped.

And that which gives you to be sensible of him, and to know him is that which convinceth you in your hearts of sin and unrighteousness, and would have you to feel after him and worship him in spirit, and serve him and live in peace; who hath promised that he will give Christ Jesus for a covenant of Light and peace. This is Christ, the second Adam, which brings the sons and daughters of Adam into reconciliation with God again, and destroys sin, and finishes it.

G. F. 1672

To Friends at Jamaica

Friends,

We do hear that some, professing Truth amongst you, do not keep to your Meetings as diligently as they ought to do, nor yet meet but few of you together upon the First Days. And the reason is, that upon the First Days some of you write and make up your accounts, so as you cannot have time to go to the Meetings! Truly, Friends, this is an ill savour to come over here into England, and shows that you mind your own business more than the Lord's, and the things of this life more than the things that appertain to the life that is without end, which should be sought for first, if you desire to be blessed and prosper. For you that have seen the order of Truth in England, how can you go out of the practice of it, without growing wild and withering?

And [see] that all Friends may be invited to the Meetings, and that you may be good examples and patterns unto all in the island in righteous dealings and doings, in weights and measures. And keep to the sound language, and the honour that you have received from above; so that your lives and conversations may preach in virtue, righteousness and holiness, and that God may be glorified through you and among you. And owe nothing to any man but love.

When you have got up your Meetings, see that nothing be lacking among you; then send over how things are with you, how Truth spreads and prospers. *So no more but my love.*

                                          G. F. 1673

Friends,

To all Friends that live in the Truth, and by it are become God's freemen and women, and by the truth and power of God are brought out of the world's vain fashions and customs, in their feastings and revellings, and banquets and wakes, and other vain feastings, where they spoil the creatures, and dishonour God more those times and days, which they call holy days and feast days, than [on] any other times and days; and therefore you that are brought out of such things, and do see the folly and vanity of them, you see their vanity, and folly and madness in their destroying the creatures, to the reproach of Christianity and the dishonour of God, and many times through the abusing of themselves by excess [they] are more like beasts than men. And therefore [because] you cannot observe their evil customs, that vain spirit [in them] is in a great rage and fury.

I say to you, mind and practise Christ's words, as you may read in *Luke* 13:14. And therefore, as you have forsaken all the world's vain feastings, and dinners, and suppers, (if so), give to the blind, the lame, the maimed, the widow, the fatherless, and the poor, a feast or a dinner, and obey Christ the heavenly man's doctrine, though it do cross old earthly Adam's will and practices; and though he be angry, never heed him, but obey the Lord.

G. F. 1673

To Friends in Virginia

Dear Friends,

To whom is my love, I am glad to hear of the increase of Truth amongst you; and the Lord prosper his work, and increase people in his knowledge. In the name [of Jesus] keep your Men's and Women's Meetings, that you may feel him in the midst of you, exercising his offices.

I am glad to hear of some of your diligence, in taking that great journey to Carolina through the woods; for if you visit them sometimes it would do well. And there is a people in that place you call New-Country, as you go to Carolina, which had a great desire to see me; amongst whom I had a Meeting. I received letters, giving me an account of the service some of you had, with and amongst the Indian King and his council. And if you go over again to Carolina, you may enquire of Capt. Batts, the old Governor, with whom I left a paper to be read to the Emperor, and his thirty kings under him of the Tusrowres, who were come to treat for peace with the people of Carolina, whether he did read it to them or no. Remember me to Major General Benett, and Col. Dew, and the rest of the Justices that were friendly and courteous to me when I was there, and came to Meetings. And tell them, that I cannot but remember their civility and moderation, when I was amongst them.

And so the Lord redouble it into your hearts and theirs, the love and kindness which they and you showed unto me. I have been a prisoner here about these eight months, and now I am praemunired, because I cannot take an oath; but the Lord's Seed and Power is over all, blessed be his name for ever, and glory and honour to him who is over all and worthy of all.

Read this amongst Friends in their Meetings.

G. F.

Worcester, 1673

(Given forth in the time of his sickness in Worcester Prison, 1674).

My dear Friends in England and all parts of the world,

The gospel, which is the power of God, which you received from the beginning, keep in it, and the fellowship of it, in which there is neither sect, nor schism, but an everlasting fellowship, and an everlasting order; which gospel brings life and immortality to light in every one of your hearts, and lets you see over him that hath darkened you. Now, I say, you that be heirs of Christ, possess him, and walk in him; and as you have received him, so walk all in peace and love, and live in his worship in the Spirit and Truth.

And you have known the manner of my life, the best part of thirty years; since I went forth and forsook all things, I sought not myself, I sought you and his glory that sent me, and when I turned you to him that is able to save you, I left you to him. And my travels hath been great, in hungers and colds, when there were few, for the first six or seven years; that I often lay in woods and commons in the night; that many times it was as a by-word that I would not come into any of their houses, and lie in their beds; and the prisons have been made my home a great part of my time, and in danger of my life, and in jeopardy daily. And amongst you I have made myself of no reputation, to keep the Truth up in reputation, as you all very well know it, that be in the fear of God. With the low, I made myself low, and with the weak and feeble, I was as one with them, and condescended to all conditions, for the Lord had fitted me so before he sent me forth. And so I passed through great sufferings in my body, as you have been sensible.

And few at the first took care of the establishing Men and Women's Meetings, though they were generally owned when they understood them; but the everlasting God, that sent me forth by his everlasting power, first to declare his everlasting gospel, and then, after people had received the gospel, I was moved to go through the nation to advise them to set up the Men's Meetings and the Women's; many of which were set up. And this was the end: that all that had received the gospel might be the possessors of it, and that all that had received Christ Jesus might so walk in him, and possess his government in the Church; and men and women, being the heirs of Christ, might inherit his order in the everlasting gospel, and now in the restoration may all be helps-meet [=help mates] in holiness and righteousness.

G. F. 1674

LETTER 106 ⸲ Ep. 314

To all my dear Friends, elect and precious, in America

Friends,

Stand fast in the faith which Christ Jesus is the author of, by his heavenly ensign, in your heavenly armour; and so stand, feeling and seeing God's banner of love over your heads, manifesting that you are the good ground, that God's Seed hath taken root downward in, and springs upward in, and brings forth fruits in, some sixty, and some hundred-fold in this life, to the praise and glory of God, always beholding the Sun of righteousness, that never sets, ruling the supernatural day, of which you are the children; and the persecutors' sun, (the heat of it which rises and sets again), cannot scorch your blade, [as] it may do that seed that grows on the stony ground.

And hold fast the hope which anchors the soul, which is sure and steadfast, that you may float above the world's sea; for your anchor holds sure and steadfast in the bottom, let the winds, storms and raging waves rise never so high. And your star is fixed, by which you may steer to the eternal land of rest, and kingdom of God. So, *no more but my love to you all.*

G. F.

Swarthmore in Lancashire, the 12th of the 12th Month, 1675.

To Friends in Barbadoes

Dear Friends, to whom is my love in the holy Truth,

My desire is that you may all be valiant for it against all deceit, that the camp of God may be kept clean, and all may be faithful in your testimonies.

Great persecutions are in most counties in England, and many are imprisoned in many places, and their goods spoiled. And we had a very large Yearly Meeting here, and very peaceable and quiet and the Lord's power and presence was richly manifest in our Meetings; and the Lord wonderfully supports Friends in all their trials and sufferings; and Friends generally are in much love and unity one with another.

Now Friends, we desire that at your Quarterly Meeting you may write over an epistle to the Yearly Meeting in London of the affairs of the Church of Christ, and the prosperity, and the spreading of his Truth there; for we had a large epistle from the Half-Yearly Meeting in Ireland, which declares Friends were all in unity there, and likewise an account was given from Scotland, and from Holland, and Freezland, Germany and other places. But at Embden and Dantzick they are under great persecution. And we have lately a new Meeting set up beyond Holland, who have been under much sufferings and persecutions, but they stand faithful to the Lord. And at Algier, in the Turks' country, Friends there have set up a Meeting amongst themselves (which are captives), about twenty Friends; and some other of the captives have been convinced at that Meeting.

And one Thomas Tilby, a captive Friend, hath a testimony for God, and speaks among them; and their patroons, or masters, lets them meet. And one of their masters spoke to a Friend, as he was going to Meeting, and thought he had been going to a public tippling-house, and he stopped him, and asked him whither he was going. And he told him, to worship the great God. And he said it was well, and let him go. And some of the

Turks said they had some among them of their people that would not buy stolen goods. I have written a large epistle to them to encourage them, and that they might preach the gospel abroad in those parts, both in their words, lives, and conversations; and this Meeting there, among the Turks, may be of great service.

And now Friends, all be careful of God's glory, and seek the good one of another; and strive to be of one mind and heart, and that the peace and gentle wisdom of God may order you all. And be courteous, kind and tender-hearted one to another.

And Friends, you may send a copy of this to the Caribee Islands.

G. F. 1675

LETTER 108 ·   of 77.   Ep. 319

To Friends in Nevis, and the Caribee Islands

Dear Friends,

I have seen a letter from some of you, wherein I understand there has been some scruple concerning watching, or sending forth watch-men in your own way.

Truly, Friends, this I declare to you, that it is a great mercy of the Lord, to subject the Governor's mind so much by his power and truth that he will permit you to watch in your own way, without carrying arms, which is a very civil thing, and to be taken notice of. For, could Friends obtain the same in Jamaica and other places they would willingly have done it, and did profer themselves for to do it to the Governors. But because that they would not bring swords, and guns, and other arms to watch against the Spaniards, as they pretended, their standing fine was about 17s. for each man's neglect, but they often took 30s. worth for it, and tied some of them neck and heels besides, till the blood hath come forth at their mouths, nose, and ears. And this I have seen upon record. And in other places it hath been the same.

Now, as for watching in itself: don't you watch your plantations against thieves in the night? And are not common watches set to discover thieves in the towns, or house-breakers, or such as wickedly fire houses? Such civil things we were subject to, and do submit ourselves, for conscience sake, unto every such ordinance of man which are for the punishment of evil-doers, and for the praise of them that do well.

Now those evil-doers that may rob your plantations, or houses, you complain to the magistrates for the punishment of them, though you cannot swear against them. Or if the Indians come to rob your plantations or houses, you complain to the magistrates for the punishment of such evil-doers, to stop them. Which magistrates are for the praise of them that do well. So this watching is for the preventing thieves and murderers, and stopping burning of houses. So we do submit to every such ordinance of man for the Lord's sake, for the Apostle exhorted to submission, so far we can obey them, in the Lord's power and truth, as they act against the evil, and that which dishonours God; and if they act against the good, or if they would compel us to those things which is matter of conscience in us towards God, we resist not, but suffer under them.

Rulers are not to be a terror to the good workers, but to the evil. But when the magistrate turns his sword backwards upon the just and righteous, then he abuses his power. You are not to be the revengers, for he is the revenger; and to that power that executes the revenge we must be subject, not only for wrath, but for conscience sake; which is for the punishment of the evil-doers, and for the praise of them that do well. For if any should come to burn your house, or rob you, or ravish your wives or daughters, or a company should come to fire a city or town, or come to kill people, don't you watch against all such actions? And won't you watch against such evil things in the power of God in your own way? You cannot but discover such things to the magistrates, who are to punish such things, and therefore the watch is kept and set up to discover such to the magistrate, that they may be punished; and if he does it not, then he bears his sword in vain. So if thou watches thy own plantation against thieves, in thy own way, which thou art desired, for the good of thyself and thy neighbours, against such as would burn thy plantation, and thy neighbour's, and destroy and rob you, wilt thou not discover this to the magistrates, to punish such evil-doers, who is set for the punishing of the evil-doers and executing wrath upon them, and for the praise of them that do well? Surely, yes.

And for this cause we pay tribute to them, and give Caesar his due, that we may live a godly and peaceable life under them.

So with my love to all Friends in those parts, as though I named them; and be at peace one with another; neither judge one another about such things, but live in love, which does edify. And give no occasion to your adversaries, neither in your lives nor in your words; but that you may all serve God in the new life, showing forth that you are new men and that you are renewed in the image of God, and that you are born again of the immortal heavenly Seed. And so be valiant for God's truth upon the earth, and spread it abroad. Preach Christ and his kingdom, his grace, his truth to men, that all should walk in it.

And much I could write to you concerning these things, but I have not been very well; but, blessed be the Lord God, his ever-lasting Seed is over all, and my life is in it.

G. F.

Swarthmore, the 5th of the 9th Month, 1675

An encouragement to all the faithful Women's Meetings in the world

Friends,

You may read in the old world how one family after another served the Lord God. You may see man and woman were helps-meet in Paradise; and after Moses received the Law, men and women in the time of the Law were helps meet again to each other in the work and service of the holy things.

And now, must not all receive the grace, and believe in the Light, and receive this gospel, and walk and labour in it, both men and women? And so now the end of all our Men and Women's Meetings in the time of the gospel (the power of Christ being the authority of them) is that they might all labour in his Power and in his Grace, and in his Light, to do his service, and his business in truth and righteousness.

So the women are to look into their own selves and families, and to look to the training up of their children; for they are oft times more amongst them than the men, and may prevent things that fall out, and many times they may make or mar their children in their education. So now they come to be exercised in the grace of God, and to admonish, and exhort, reprove, and rebuke, and keep all their families modest, honest, virtuous, sober and civil, and not to give liberty, nor indulge that which tends to vice.

Now when the women are met together in the Light, and in the gospel, the power of God, some are of more large capacity and understanding than other women, and are able to inform, and instruct, and stir up others into diligence, virtue, and righteousness, and godliness, and to help them that be of weaker capacities, that they may be fruitful in every good work and word.

Some there have been that would not have the women to speak without the men; and some of them say the women must not speak in the Church. And if they must not speak, what should they meet with them for? What a spirit is this, that will neither suffer the women to speak amongst the men, nor to meet amongst themselves to speak? For the power and spirit of God gives liberty to all; for women are heirs of life as well as the men, and heirs of Grace, and of the Light of Christ Jesus, as well as the men, and so stewards of the manifold grace of God.

And now, you that stumble at Women's Meetings, had not your women many vain meetings before they were convinced? And you were not then offended at them. And when they had junketing meetings to themselves did you reprove them for such meetings? And why should they not meet now in their conversion in the Lord's power and spirit, to do his business, wherein men and women may be helps-meet in the religion that is not of this world?

And some have said that such Meetings must not be, but as business or occasion requires them. As much as to say, you must not make up the hedges till the beasts have devoured your corn, and then the parish overseers must meet together to compute the damage, as if it were not more their duty to meet to prevent bad actions that may fall out, and with the power of God to stop up gaps to prevent evil or weak places. For when the evil is entered into, it is of the latest to meet then, which rather brings scandal than remedy; and therefore the labourers in the gospel (men and women) are to see that all live and walk in the order of the gospel, and to see that nothing be lacking: for the women in their assemblies may inform one another of the poor widows and fatherless, and in the wisdom of God may find the best way for the setting forth of their children, and to see that their children are preserved in the Truth, and instruct them in the fear of the Lord. And if there were no Scripture for our Men and Women's Meetings, Christ is sufficient, who restores men and women up to the image of God.

G. F.

Marsh-grainge, the 16th of the 9th Month, 1676.

To Friends at Dantzick

Dear Friends,

In the love of God, and the Lord Jesus Christ, look above all your outward sufferings, and him that is out of Truth that makes you to suffer, and let nothing separate you from the love of God which you have in Christ Jesus. I say, let not carnal weapons, gaols, and prisons, threats or reproaches move you, but feel the well of life springing up in you, to nourish the plant that God has planted in you. And therefore let your faith stand in the Lord's power, which is your hedge and defence. And so to the praise and glory of God you may bring forth fresh and green fruit, being grafted into the Green Tree, that never withers.

O, be valiant for God's glory and his truth upon the earth, and spread it abroad, answering that of God in every man's and woman's conscience; knowing him that hath brought everlasting peace into the earth, that the songs of salvation may be in your mouths. So every true believer will confess to Christ his salvation, their way, their Light, and Life, out of death and darkness: their prophet to open to them; their shepherd, to feed them; and their bishop, to oversee them; their captain and commander, to command and to lead them; and their priest, who hath offered himself for them, and also sanctifies them and offers them up to God. To whom be all praise and glory for ever, Amen.

I writ something to the magistrates, which is in print in England; which, if you have it not to give them, you may send into Holland, and let it be translated into your language and given to them, and spread it up and down in your country.

So, in that love which bears all things, and keeps your hearts, minds, and souls up to God, through which you come to love God, and Christ and one another: in that live and dwell.

G. F.

Swarthmore, the 17th of the 3rd Month, 1676.

To Friends in New Jersey in America

My dear Friends in New Jersey, and you that go to New Jersey,

My desire is that you may all be kept in the fear of God, and that you may have the Lord in your eye, in all your undertakings: for many eyes of other governments or colonies will be upon you; yea, the Indians, to see how you order your lives and conversations. And therefore let your lives, and words, and conversations be as becomes the gospel, that you may adorn the Truth, and honour the Lord in all your undertakings. Let that only be in your eye, and you will have the Lord's blessing and increase, both in basket and field, and store-house; and at your lyings-down you will feel him, and at your goings-forth, and comings-in.

And keep up your Meetings for Worship. And after you are settled, you may join together, and build a Meeting House. And do not strive about outward things, but dwell in the love of God, for that will unite you together, and make you kind and gentle one towards another; and to seek one another's good and welfare; and to see that nothing be lacking among you; and then all will be well.

And write over yearly, from your Meetings how you are settled, and how your affairs go in the Truth, and how your Men and Women's Meetings are settled. And my desires are that we may hear you are a good savour to God in those countries, so that the Lord may crown all your actions with his glory. So with my love to all.

G. F.

Swarthmore, the 4th of the 1st Month, 1676.

My dear Friends,

To whom is my love in the everlasting Seed, that reigns over all, and will overcome all your persecutors, and the Devil, that is the cause thereof, who fighteth against the Light (which is the Life in Christ), as they did against him in the flesh, above sixteen hundred years ago.

And now my Friends, suffer as lambs in the time of your sufferings; let your wills be subjected with the patience that hath the victory, and run the race, and obtain the crown of life; and be willing to suffer for Christ's sake. So nothing is overcome by any man's will, but by faith that giveth access to God, in which they please God; and I do believe that all your sufferings will be for good for your establishing upon the holy rock of Life, which was the rock of all the sufferers, the prophets, and the apostles; who is the anointed saviour, to the answering that of God in all people: for the Lord hath a great work and Seed in that place.

And so, in love to God, and in love to your persecutors, you can pray for them who persecute you; and this suffering is above all the sufferings in the world, which are without love and charity, who maketh one another to suffer when they get the upper hand; but such are not the sufferers for the true Lord Jesus who suffered; though he was above all, yet he made none to suffer; and when he was reviled, he reviled not again, but said, 'Father forgive them'.

G. F.

The 18th of the 5th Month, 1677.

Friends,

Know what the Lord doth require of you, and all have a sense of that in yourselves: which is, to do justly, and to love mercy, and to walk humbly with God. Now the Lord who is merciful and just, holy and righteous, pure and perfect, doth require that man and woman should do justly and righteously, and live godlily and holily, by the holy Light and Spirit, and Truth and Grace, that the Lord hath given every man and woman to profit withal. And so to answer the holy, pure righteous just God of Truth in all their lives and words and conversations; and so to glorify him upon the earth. And the more the Lord gives, the more he requireth; and the less that he giveth, the less he requireth. But the Lord requireth of every man and woman as he giveth; who will judge the world by the man Christ Jesus, according to the gospel, the power of God, that is preached to every creature under heaven; that is, according to the invisible Power; manifesting that there is something of the invisible power of God in every man and woman.

So according to his Grace, and Light and gospel will the righteous God judge the world in righteousness, by Christ the heavenly and spiritual man, who hath died for the sins of the world; though they deny him that bought them. Such deserve his judgement.

Send this abroad among Friends, to be read in their Meetings.

                                                                    G. F.

Swarthmore, the 11th Month, 1678.

My dear Friends,

Whose faces are set towards Zion, from this dung-hill world of vanity and vexation of spirit, the glory, comfort and pleasures of which pass away, they that have more or less of it and that enter into it, enter into trouble; and when they are in it, it is a great trouble to come out of it, and to be a fool for Christ's sake, who is not of this world, but of the world that hath no end. And therefore you must believe in the Light, Grace and Truth that cometh from him, in the inward parts or heart, which directeth your minds to Christ, from whence this comes, and to unite to him that is heavenly, who saith 'Seek the Kingdom of God first'; then all outward things will be added to them that have found the Kingdom of God, that standeth in righteousness, and in the power of God, and in peace and joy in the Holy Ghost; and the good Seed are the children of this kingdom, which is everlasting.

And take heed of your wills, and give not way to them, but give way to the power and spirit of God, which crucifieth [them], and keeps [them] under the Cross of Christ; so that your inward man may be renewed, and the old Adam put off; so that the Day Light of Jesus Christ may be seen, [which they rejoice to see] that see the sun of righteousness shine in their hearts, to nourish that which God hath there planted, who watereth it with the living water of the Word, his living plant.

What is the matter that all the world is of so many ways since the apostles' days? Because they are out of Christ, the Way, the new and living Way (which is over all the dead ways), which was set up above sixteen hundred years ago. And why have they so many religions? Because they are out of the pure and undefiled religion of God, and gone into them of their own making, and do not worship God, as Christ taught above sixteen hundred years ago, in Spirit and in Truth.

So all must come to the spirit and truth in their own hearts and souls, if they do know the God of Truth. And my desire is that you in your measures may be preserved to the Lord, and know what he doth require of you, to love mercy, to do justice, and to walk humbly with God, who will judge the world in righteousness, according to the gospel preached in every creature, showing that there is something of God in every creature that shall answer his judgement.

And therefore my desire is that all may be faithful to what the Lord hath made known unto them by his Grace, and Truth, and Light, Power and Spirit; and then the Lord will supply them with more. To whom be glory and praise, who is the creator of all, through Jesus Christ, by whom all things were made, Amen.

G. F. 1678

LETTER 115 •   Ep. 355

To Friends in America, concerning their Negroes and Indians

All Friends every where, that have Indians or Blacks,

You are to preach the gospel to them, and other servants, if you be true Christians, for the gospel of salvation was to be preached to every creature under heaven. Christ commands it to his disciples, 'Go and teach all nations, baptising them in the name of the Father, Son, and Holy Ghost.' And this is the one baptism with the spirit into one body.

And also you must preach the grace of God to all Blacks and Indians, which Grace brings salvation, that hath appeared unto all men, to teach them to live godly, righteously, and soberly. Which grace of God is sufficient to teach and establish all true Christians, that they may appear before the throne of grace.

And also, you must instruct all Blacks and Indians, and others, how that God doth pour out of his spirit upon all flesh in these days of the new covenant, and new Testament; and that none of them must quench the motions of his spirit, nor grieve it, nor vex it, nor rebel against it, nor err from it, but be led by his good spirit to instruct them; with which they may profit in the things of God.

And also you must teach them all how that Christ by the grace of God tasted death for every man, and gave himself a ransom for all men, to be testified in due time, and is the propitiation not for the sins of Christians only, but for the sins of the whole world.

And Christ, who is the Light of the world, saith 'Believe in the Light that ye may become children of the Light'. And they that do evil and hate the Light will not come into the Light, because it will reprove them, and be their condemnation; and if they do not believe, they will be reproved, condemned and judged by Christ, who hath all power to judge and reward every man according to his works, whether they be good or evil.

And therefore you are to open the promises of God to the ignorant: how God would give Christ a new covenant, a Light to the Gentiles and the heathen, and that he is God's salvation to the ends of the earth, and how that the earth shall be covered with the knowledge of the Lord as the waters cover the sea, so that the glorious knowledge of the Lord should cover the earth. And so through Christ Jesus man and woman comes again to God. All blessings and praises be to the Lord God, through Jesus Christ, for ever and ever more. Amen.

G. F.

Swarthmore, the 10th Month, 1679.

Dear Friends,

With my love to you in the holy peaceable Truth that never changes, nor admits of no evil, but makes all free that receive it and that walk in it. And from the Truth floweth justice, equity, righteousness and godliness, mercy and tenderness, that brings man's heart, mind, soul and spirit to the infinite and incomprehensible God. And from [the Truth] a love flows to all the universal creation, and would have all come to the knowledge of the Truth, and it bends everyone to their utmost ability to serve God and his Truth, and to spread it abroad, and it brings their minds out of the earth, which makes them brittle and changeable.

As to *unity:* it makes all like itself, that do obey it; [and] *Universal,* to live out of narrowness and self, and deny it. So it brings all into oneness, and answereth the good principle of God in all people, and brings into humility, and the fear of the Lord, which is the beginning of wisdom, and it brings all to have a care of God's glory and his honour.

The Lord, who is the God of all peace and order, alone protects and preserves his people with his eternal power; for the Devil's power is not eternal: it had a beginning, and must have an ending. And therefore, Friends, patience must be exercised in the Truth; and keep to the word of patience.

So with my love in the Seed of Life, that reigns over all.

G. F. 1679

And now, my dear Friends, concerning True Liberty

The true liberty is in the gospel, the power of God. And in this gospel is the Saints' fellowship, which the Devil with all his false fellowships cannot get into, for it is a mystery.

Likewise true Liberty is in the Faith, which Jesus Christ is the author and finisher of, which gives victory over that which separates man and woman from God, and by which they have access to God again.

And therefore all ye Friends of Christ Jesus, stand fast in the liberty wherewith Christ hath made you free, by his Light, Grace, Truth, Spirit, Faith and everlasting Gospel, the everlasting power of God.

And now, ye babes of Christ, if the world do hate you, it hated Christ your Lord and master also; if they do mock, and reproach, and defame and buffet you, they did so to your Lord and master also, who was and is the Green Tree, that gives nourishment to all his branches, his followers.

G. F. 1679

A Letter to the captives who met together to worship God in Algier

Dear Friends,

I understand from a letter from a Friend, a captive amongst you, dated the 20th of the 10th Month, 1681, that you have a Meeting there in Algier of about twenty. I am glad to hear you meet, and it is very well you have such liberty from your patroons. And my desire is that the Lord may preserve you all, that do meet in the name of Jesus, that in your lives and conversations, and words, you may preach righteousness and holiness and godliness, and the life of Truth, so that you may answer the spirit of God, both in the Turks and the Moors, and in the rest of the captives, that God's city may be set upon the holy hill there which cannot be hid; but that all may see it, wherewith Christ hath enlightened every man that cometh into the world.

If Christ, I say, has led you out of prison and captivity, into the glorious liberty of the sons of God, stand fast in that liberty, and be not entangled with any yoke or bondage, to bring you out of that heavenly spiritual liberty. For in this you are free, notwithstanding the prisons and captivity of men, [for] they are but small matters to it.

So with my love to you all in the holy Seed Christ Jesus, that reigns over all from everlasting to everlasting. The Lord preserve you all tender vines in him, Amen.

G. F.

London, the 17th of the 1st Month, 1682.

To suffering Friends at Horsham in Sussex

Dear Friends,

Who suffer for your testimony, and to all the rest in your county, I am glad to hear of your faithfulness, and of your standing for the Church which Christ is the head of, which is in God, and are become his living members. And therefore wheresoever ye are, in prison, or out of prison, where two or three are gathered together in his name, there is a Church, and Christ the living Head in the midst of them: a prophet, to open to his Church the things of his Kingdom; and a bishop, to oversee his living members, that they be preserved in his Light, Grace, Truth, Spirit, and Gospel; and he is a shepherd, to feed them with heavenly food, and a priest, who has offered himself up a sacrifice for the sins of the whole world, who cleanses, washes and purifies his Church. And therefore feel and see Christ exercising his offices, and ruling in your hearts.

And now, dear Friends, my desires are, that you may all live in the love of God, and in the unity of his spirit, which is the bond of peace, in which you will all be kind and courteous one to another, and so the God of all peace and power support you, and strengthen you, and uphold you, throughout your trials and sufferings, that he may be glorified in you all.

G. F.

London, the 20th of the 12th Month, 1681.

LETTER 120   Ep. 369

To the flock of Christ Jesus every where, to be read in their Assemblies

Friends,

Christ saith, 'In me ye have peace, in the world ye have trouble'; and therefore keep out the spirit of the world. And

'Without me,' says Christ, 'ye can do nothing'; without his grace, his light, his truth, his gospel, his power, his spirit, his faith, ye can do nothing. And therefore, my Friends and brethren, both males and females, keep and walk in the Seed, in which all nations are blest, which bruises the head of the serpent, and destroys the Devil and all his works, which brought misery and the curse upon all nations. In the righteousness of Christ you may all come to walk in the new Covenant of Light, which was before the Prince of darkness was, and [in] Life, which is over death, and was before death was.

And keep in the Cross of Christ, the power of God. For if you do not keep in this power of God, to keep you crucified to the world, but let in the spirit of the world, you let in his god, which will crucify the good in you, and you will come to crucify to yourselves the Son of God afresh, and put him to open shame.

And now, all Friends and brethren, let your meekness, your temperance, and your gentleness and sobriety, and tenderness, and moderation appear to all men, that your Light may so shine that they may see your good works, and glorify your Father which is in heaven.

And keep out of the restless, discontented, disquieted spirit of the world about the government; for you know it has always been our way to seek the good of all, and to live peaceably under the government, and to seek their eternal good, peace and happiness in the Lord Jesus Christ; and to lay our innocent sufferings before them, who have made no resistance but have prayed for them that persecuted us, and despitefully used us, according to the command of Christ.

G. F.

The 21st of the 9th Month, 1681.

To Friends in New Jersey and Pennsylvania

Dear Friends,

With my love to you all, in God's holy peaceable Truth, and my desires are that you may all be kept careful of God's glory. Now in your settling of plantations and provinces, and especially in woody countries, you may have many trials and troubles, but if you keep in the wisdom of God, that will keep you both gentle, and kind, and easy to be entreated one of another, and that will preserve you out of heats, or extremes, or passions.

And I desire that you may be very kind and courteous to all in necessity, in the love of God; for there are many people goes over to your countries, some poor and some rich; and so, many eyes are upon you. And therefore my desire is that you may all be careful in the love of God, and in his truth and righteousness, as the family of God, and be careful and tender to all your servants in all respects.

And dear Friends, I desire that you would send over an account by the next ship how many Meetings you have, and let us know how Truth spreads and prospers amongst you; which you would do well to write every year, to the Yearly Meeting at London.

G. F. 1682

To Friends that are prisoners at York

Dear Friends,

With my love to you all, and all the rest of the faithful Friends in bonds; and my desire is to the Lord that ye all may stand faithful and valiant for his glorious name, and his holy peaceable Truth now in this day of storm and tempest, that none may turn their backs on the Lord in this day of trial, and none be ashamed of confessing of Christ.

Mind the Lord in all your sufferings, and keep all low, and in the humility of heart, and there you will feel that he that inhabits eternity dwells with an humble heart; and he will be your shield and buckler, and defender in time of trouble; and therefore do not think time long, and your sufferings long, for the Lord will lay no more upon you, but what you are able to bear. I know it, and am a witness for God in all my sufferings and imprisonments, and halings before magistrates about sixty times, about this thirty-six year. And so, Friends, when you are tried, you may come forth more precious than gold that is tried in the fire.

And though you be in outward bonds from your wives, families, houses and relations, yet the word of God is not bound: It's at liberty; it abides and endures for ever. It will make you all rich, though they think to make you poor with their bonds, and cast you into prisons, but I tell you, the word of God will make you rich, for the word of God was before the wicked and his bonds were; for in the beginning was the word, but since the beginning was the Devil.

In Christ you have heavenly peace: that none can take away from you. In him live and dwell.

G. F. 1682

Friends,

My friends that are gone, and are going over to plant, and make outward plantations in America, keep your own plantations in your hearts, with the spirit and power of God. And in all places where you do outwardly live and settle, invite all the Indians, and their kings, and have Meetings with them, or they with you, so that you may make inward plantations with the light and power of God, and the grace and truth and spirit of Christ; and that with it you may answer the Light and Truth and Spirit of God in the Indians, their kings and people, and so by it you may make heavenly plantations in their hearts for the Lord, and so beget them to God that they may serve and worship him, and spread his Truth abroad.

And so that you may all be kept warm in God's love and power and zeal for the honour of his name.

G. F.

London, the 22nd of the 9th Month, 1682.

All my dearly beloved Friends and Brethren every where,

The Lord God Almighty with his holy spirit and power hath gathered and kept and preserved you to this day a people to himself. And now, dear Friends, in all your words, in all your business and employments, have a care of breaking your words and promises to any people; but that you may (before you make promises to any man or woman) consider beforehand, that you may be able to perform and fulfil both your words and promises to all people, and that your *yea* be *yea,* and *nay, nay,* in all things, which Christ hath set up instead of an oath.

G. F.

Edmonton, in the County of Middlesex, the 23rd of the 11th Month, 1682.

A way to prevent the indignation and judgements of God from coming on a kingdom, nation, or family

First, all you vintners, and you inn-keepers, see that you never let any man or woman have more wine, ale, or other strong liquors, than what is for their health and their good, that they may praise God for his good creatures. For every creature of God is good and ought to be received with thanksgiving.

But if you do let men or women have so much strong drink, till they be drunk,

1. You destroy the good creatures of God.
2. You destroy them that have not power over their lusts, no more than a rat or a swine, who will drink till they are drunk.
3. You are a great cause of ruining them in their healths, purses, and estates (their children and families) in feeding of them in their lusts, by letting them have more than doth them good; which also tends to bring God's judgements upon you, to your own ruin and destruction.

For many, when they are full of wine, beer, or strong liquor will call for music, pipe and harp, (and it may be their whores also). And so in this, you that suffer or allow such things are nurses of debauchery, and corrupters of them, and of your own families also.

And also such men, when they are full of strong drink, and have destroyed the creatures by taking more than doth them good, then they are got to that height that they are ready to quarrel and abuse, or kill or destroy one another; and sometimes kill other people (who do them no harm), as they are walking or travelling in the streets or highways.

This testimony and warning was and is owned and subscribed to by many vintners and other, concerned in the trades and callings before-mentioned, who were present at the reading of the manuscript.

G. F. 1682

To Friends in Charleston in Carolina

Dear Friends,

I received your letter dated the 6th day of the 8th Month, 1683, wherein you give an account of your Meeting, and of your liberty in your province, which I am glad to hear of, though your Meeting is but small. But, however, stand all faithful in truth and righteousness, that your fruits may be unto holiness, and your end will be everlasting life [and] that to all people in that dark wilderness you may answer the Truth both in them that are called Christians, and in the Indians. And my desire is that you may prize your liberty, both natural and spiritual, and the favour that the Lord hath given you, that your *yea* is taken instead of an oath, and that you do serve both in Assemblies, juries, and other offices, without swearing, according to the doctrine of Christ. Which is a great thing worth prizing.

For we are here under great persecution. Betwixt thirteen and fourteen hundred in prison, an account of which hath lately been delivered to the King, besides great spoil and havoc which is made of Friends' goods, and besides many are imprisoned and praemunired for not swearing allegiance. And we are kept out of our Meetings in streets and highways in many places of the land, and beaten, and abused. Therefore prize the liberty which you enjoy. But the Lord's power is over all, and supports his people.

Seek the good of all, and the profit of all; and the exalting of [God's] name and truth in your day and generation; and live in the Truth and the love of it; and overcome evil with good; and hold fast to that which is good. Then you can try all things.

G. F.

London, the 23rd of the 12th Month, 1683.

To Friends that are captives at Algier

Dear Friends,

To you is my love, and to all the rest that fears God, that meets with you; my desires are that you may all keep low in humility. In the fear of God there is no danger, for God dwells with the humble, and teaches the humble the way they should walk.

Now there is a common saying amongst the Turks to the Christians, 'your crucified God', meaning Christ. Now this is their mistake. Though God was in Christ reconciling the world to himself it was not the eternal God that died, and was crucified, that was in Christ. For Christ said, when he was about to suffer, 'My God, my God, why hast thou forsaken me?' So Christ suffered in the flesh and died, and was crucified, as he was man, but not as he was God, the Word, that was in the beginning, but as he was man that bore the sins and iniquities of the whole world. So I say again that Christ did not die as he was God, but as man. He was crucified and buried, and rose again on the third day, and ascended, and is at the right hand of God. This he did by the power of God, as he was man. So the Turks are mistaken to say or to think that the eternal God could be crucified or die.

Dear Friends, I thought it needful to write a letter to you concerning this their mistake, which you may be wise in making use of. And my desires are that you may be preserved, and exalt God's name in your places of captivity. I think you have more liberty than we have here, for they keep us out of our Meetings, and cast us into prisons, and spoil our goods. And therefore prize your liberty in your Meetings, and do not abuse it.

Read this openly in your Meetings; and I have sent you here some books that you may read them, or give them to the Turks or English, as you see fit.

And Friends, it would be very well for you if you could get the

Turks' or Moors' language, that you might be the more enabled to direct them to the grace and spirit of God in them. And then, getting their language, you would be able to write and translate any papers to them.

G. F.

Gousey, in Essex, the 10th of the 2nd Month, 1683.

LETTER 128 ·   Ep. 389

Friends,

It's desired, that all Friends, that have children, families, and servants, may train them up in the pure and unspotted religion, and in the nurture and fear of God, and that frequently they may read the holy Scriptures, which is much better than to be gadding abroad. And exhort and admonish them that every family apart may serve and worship the Lord, as well as in public. And that when they go to Meetings they may take their families and servants with them, that they may not go wandering up and down in the fields, or to ale-houses, as many have done, to the dishonour of God, and to the dishonour of their masters' and mistresses' families, and to their own ruin and destruction. And therefore, for Christ's sake, and his pure religion, let there be care taken to prevent all these things. For such a one as cannot rule well his own house, having his children in subjection with all due gravity, how can he take care of the church of God?

And now, Friends, concerning marriages, of which very many things have been written, it's desired that all may be careful in that thing of running hastily together. And consider it first, as it is God's joining, so it is his ordinance, and it is honourable in all, and the bed undefiled. And again, consider, such men as draw out young women's affections, and run from one to another, and leave them and run to others; and such women as draw out

122

men's affections, and then leave them, and draw out other men's affections. These practices bring many young men and many young women into trouble, and are sharply to be reproved. For this work is not of God's joining. Some of you have gone so far as to promises, espousals and contracts, and then left them and gone to others. This is to be judged and reproved, for as we make no contract for marriages, we break none.

And likewise such as, after they are married, break their covenant in marriage, such go from the spirit of God, and his joining, and from the spiritual society of God's people, and their unity and fellowship. Such are to be reproved by the spirit of God, and if they do not return after reproof, Friends cannot have unity or fellowship with them, though they may have the form of godliness, and have been called a sister or a brother.

G. F. 1683

LETTER 129 ·   Ep. 396

To the suffering Friends of Dantzick

Friends,

With my love in the Lord Jesus Christ to you, who is your saviour and prophet, that God hath raised up for you, to hear in all things.

Now, dear Friends, we do hear and understand that the Magistrates have cast you into prison again in Dantzick; and that they have proferred you your liberty, upon condition that you would go away, or forsake your common Meeting place, or divide yourselves into several little Meetings. Truly, Friends, we have had many of these profers made to us within this twenty or thirty years, but we never durst make such bargains or covenants to forsake the assembling of ourselves together as we used to do, but did leave our suffering cause wholly to the Lord Christ Jesus, in whose name we were gathered. And the Lord at last did and hath tendered the hearts of many of our prosecutors both in England and other places. And therefore in the spirit and power of the Lord Jesus Christ it is good to be faithful, who is God all-sufficient to support and supply you all in whatever you do. For if they should get a little advantage upon you, and get you into weakness, it would not rest so, but get more upon you. And therefore it is good to stand fast in the liberty in Christ Jesus.

And now, dear Friends, I desire, however, that you walk wisely, and lovingly, and meekly, and soberly to all the Magistrates, and all people, that they may have no just occasion in any thing against you. For the good must overcome the bad, as the apostle says.

And now, dear Friends, you that have stood such hard and cruel sufferings so long, for the Lord's name and truth, and could not be overcome by cruelty, take heed now lest you be overcome by fair words and flattery, for in that is a greater danger.

G. F. 1684

LETTER 130 ·   Ep. 399

Concerning the pure and undefiled religion, that was set up above sixteen hundred years ago

Dear Friends,

You, who profess the Light, Faith, Grace and Spirit of Christ, and the pure undefiled religion before God the Father, are to keep yourselves unspotted from the world. The Light of Christ letteth you see the spots of the world, and the grace of God will teach you to deny them, and the spirit of Truth, if you be led by it, teacheth you to mortify and subdue them.

Take heed of greediness, and earthly mindedness, and

covetousness. And take heed of unrighteousness in your trades, commerces or dealings, and take heed of over-reaching, and using deceit; and take heed of profaneness, looseness and evil words, which corrupt good manners. And take heed of drunkenness, theft, murder, whoredom, adultery, and all manner of uncleanness; and take heed of lying and swearing and cursing. For all they which act such things are void of the pure unspotted religion, and they are blotted and spotted with the actions of the world that lieth in wickedness, and their religion is vain.

And all such as follow the lust of the eye, the pride of life, and the lust of the flesh, [and are] the proud, vain, lofty, scornful, are void of the pure religion.

And take heed of malice, hatred, envy, wrath. These are the spots of the world, contrary to the spirit of meekness, gentleness, kindness, sobriety, love and mercifulness, which are the fruits of the pure spirit of God, which leadeth to the pure undefiled religion. Happy had all Christendom been, if they had kept to this pure undefiled religion to this day, and then they would not have made so many religions.

And this is the pure undefiled religion that all Christians should be of, which is from one God the creator of all. So, there is one God, the creator of all, and one Lord Jesus Christ, who is the mediator betwixt God and man; even the Man Christ Jesus. There is one body, and one spirit, even as you are called to one hope, and one God and Father of all, who is above you all; and in you all, and through you all; and there is one faith, which Christ Jesus is the author and finisher of; and there is one baptism, and by one spirit we are all baptised into one body; whether we be Jews or Gentiles, bond or free, must all drink into this one spirit of Christ, and so to keep the unity in the spirit, which is the bond of peace. For Christ said in his prayer to his Father, *that they may be all one* (meaning the true Christians), *as thou, Father, art in me, and I in thee, that they also may be one in us, that they may be one, even as we are one. I in them, and thou in me, that they may be made perfect in one.* Here you may see God and Christ are one in them (so he prayeth, that his people may be one) in whom they have rest, life, and salvation with God, through Jesus Christ.

G. F.

The 4th of the 2nd Month, 1685.

LETTER 131 ·   Ep. 405

To Friends of the ministry in Pennsylvania and New Jersey

My dear Friends, with my love to you all, and the rest of Friends,

I was glad to hear from you, but you gave me no account of the increase of Truth amongst you, nor what Meetings you have had amongst the Indian Kings and their people abroad in the countries, and of your visiting Friends in New-England, Virginia, and Carolina; nor of your travels and labours in the Gospel, who hath in all these countries liberty to serve and worship God, and to preach the Truth. And I understand that many have a desire to live in it, especially in Carolina, and that you who now travel from Friends, to Friends thither, it is thought strange that you do not visit them. Therefore I desire you may improve your gifts and talents, and not hide it under a napkin, lest it be taken from you. And my desire is that you may all be diligent, serving the Lord, and minding his glory and the prosperity of his Truth, this little time that you have to live.

And therefore, consider, that you are but sojourners here, that you may pass your time in the fear of God, and that you being many, and having many of the Friends of the ministry, you may be a hindrance unto one another if you do not travel in the Life of the universal Truth. So I desire you to be valiant for it upon the earth, that you may give a good account unto God at the last

126

with joy. So, I desire that all Friends in the ministry may see this.

And so, with my love to you all in the Holy Seed of Life that reigns over all. Amen.

G. F.

Enfield, the 30th of the 5th Month, 1685.

LETTER 132 ·   Ep. 407

To Friends in Dantzick

Dear Friends,

I am glad to hear of your welfare in the Lord.

And now, Friends, consider the Lord's great mercy and kindness towards you, who hath brought you through great sufferings, tribulations and persecutions, and that you have your Meetings peaceable. It is a great mercy of the Lord to you, for you to prize, and be faithful.

As for the affairs of Truth here, we are under great persecutions, imprisonments, and spoilings of goods; but the Lord does support his people above them all. And of late the chief Magistrates have showed some favour towards us.

G. F.

Bethnal Green, the 11th of the 9th Month, 1685.

To all the holy women that trust in God, and do profess godliness with good works

Friends,

If you do believe in the Covenant of Light, Life and Grace, then why do you not all train up your children in the same? Did not the Lord command the Jews to train up their children in the old covenant, and teach them to walk in it? So are not all you that profess the new Covenant of Grace, Light and Life, and the gospel of salvation preached to every creature, are you not to train up your children and families in this Light of the gospel and Grace of Christ which brings salvation, and brings them into favour with God, that you may have the comfort of your children in this world, and in that which is everlasting? And therefore train them up in the fear of God, and in his covenant of Light and Grace, which grace brings their salvation, and brings them into favour with God, and into the spiritual baptism, so that they may serve and worship the living God in his spirit and truth.

And if children and young people must be left, and let alone to themselves, why did the prophets and the apostles exhort the people to train up their children in the fear of the Lord, and to teach them his law when they were young, so that they might not depart from it when they were old? Therefore consider you that profess the new covenant, what care lies upon you, in your families, of teaching and instructing your servants and children? *And now, do not say but you are all warned in your life-time, and therefore prize your time while you have it, that you spend it to the honour and glory of God.*

The 9th of the 5th Month, 1685,   G. F.

To Friends in West Jersey and Pennsylvania

Dear Friends,

I am glad to hear that Truth's concerns is so well as it is with you, and that you have set up your Half Year's Meeting there, which may be of great service. For, indeed, all the faithful men and women in the power of the Lord do keep their Meetings, that they may take care of God's glory, and see that all are diligent, that profess the Truth, to walk in it; and all the loose, and such as despise dignities and the power of God, and true Christianity, should be admonished and exhorted, and not to have a name of Truth without the nature of it. And so that all may walk in the Truth, and by it come into a holy life and conversation; by that they may answer that which is good, both in the people among you, and in the Indians.

And, therefore, all that are faithful in your own country, being kept in the Lord's eternal power, in it keep up all your Men's and Women's Meetings, that the power of the Lord God may spread over all, and by it all deceit and looseness may be kept under; and this will ease all the magistrates, and their courts, of all evil and looseness, by having it stopped and killed in the birth, before it comes into action; and to see in your Meetings that Friends may give no occasion to the Indians.

And sometimes you should have Meetings with the Indian kings and their councils, to let them know the principles of Truth, so that they may know the way of salvation, and the nature of true Christianity. And so the gospel of salvation must be preached to every creature under heaven, and how that Christ hath enlightened them, who enlightens all that come into the world.

And so, now that you are settled in those parts, which have a testimony from the Lord to bear to people of the Truth, you should spread abroad God's eternal Truth. For if you should settle down in the earth, and have plenty, and be full, and at ease for a time, and not keep in the power and service, and spirit of God, you would quickly lose your condition, as some did in Rhode Island, [who] settled down in the earth, after a while, and then turned to jangling about it, and some ran out one way, and some another.

And therefore, I desire that the Lord may grant that you may all be kept and preserved by his holy Power, so that the Lord God Almighty, and his Son, may walk in the midst of you, and may delight to do you good. So with my love to all faithful Friends.

G. F.

Edmonton, the 27th of the 11th Month, 1687.

LETTER 135 ·   Ep. 417

Dear Friends and Brethren in Christ Jesus,

All walk in the power and spirit of God, that is over all, in love and unity. For Love overcomes, and builds up, and unites all the members of Christ to him the head; for Love keeps out of all strife, and is of God; and love and charity never fails, but keeps the mind above all outward things, or strife about outward things, and is that which overcomes evil, and casts out false fears, and is of God, and unites all the hearts of his people together in the heavenly joy, concord, and unity.

And the God of Love preserve you all, and settle and establish you in Christ Jesus, your life and salvation, in whom you have all peace with God. And so, walk in him, that you may be ordered in his peaceable heavenly wisdom, to the glory of God, and the comfort of one another. Amen.

G. F.

London, the 27th of the 3rd Month, 1689.

Dear Friends,

Something was upon me to write unto you, that such among Friends, who marry and provide great dinners, that instead thereof, it will be of a good savour on such occasions, that they may be put in mind at such times to give something to the poor that be widows and fatherless, and such like, to make them a feast, or to refresh them. And this I look upon would be a very good savour, to feast the poor that cannot feast you again, and would be a good practice and example. And I do really believe, that whatever they give, less or more, according to their ability, cheerfully, they will not have the less at the year's end, for the Lord loves a cheerful giver.

I know this practice hath been used by some twenty years ago. And so it is not only to give the poor a little victuals, which you cannot eat yourselves, but give them a little money, that the Lord hath blessed you withal; and give it to some of the Women's Meetings for to distribute to the poor. These things I do recommend to you (though it may look a little strange) to weigh and consider the thing. It will be both of a good report, and a good savour, and manifests a self-denial and openness of heart, and of the general love of God.

G. F.

London, the 4th of the 4th Month, 1690.

To Friends, captives at Macqueness [on the Algerian coast]

Dear Friends,

With my love to you all in the Lord Jesus Christ, in whom you have life and salvation, and rest and peace in God, though in the world troubles; and though you be in captivity from your wives and children, and relations and friends, yet the Lord is present with you by his spirit of Grace, Light and Truth. And so feel him at all times, and stand in his will. Do not murmur nor complain, but stand still in the faith and power of God, that you may see your salvation.

And it would be very well, if that you that be captives and Friends could have Meetings as they had at Algier, to the comforting and refreshing one another. And you may speak to your patroons of your meeting together to worship God that created heaven and earth, and made all mankind, and gives you breath, life, and spirit to serve and worship him.

And what do you know, but that the Lord hath set you there to preach in life and word and good conversation? Therefore while you are there, mind your service for God, who hath all things in his hand. And a sparrow cannot fall to the ground without his providence. And Christ is the mountain that filleth the whole earth, and so you will feel him there.

G. F.

London, the 25th of the 8th Month, 1690.

Postscript

You may petition the King or Emperor, and your patroons, whose captives you are, that you may have one day in the week to meet together to worship and serve the Great God (that made you) in spirit and truth. For you worship no representation, image or likeness, neither in heaven nor in the earth, but the Great God, who is Lord over all, both in heaven and earth; and is manifest by his Spirit in his people. From you, poor captives, who desire their good here, and their eternal happiness hereafter.

And you may draw up a paper to this effect, and get it translated into their language, and send it to the Emperor and his Council, and your patroons; and set your hands to it with all speed, after the receipt of this.

GEORGE FOX.

SUGGESTIONS FOR FURTHER READING

General

Christian Faith and Practice in the experience of the Society of Friends (London Yearly Meeting, 1960, £2.50).

Introducing Quakers by George H. Gorman (QHS, 1969, rptd. 1978, 60 pence).

Quaker by convincement by Geoffrey Hubbard (Penguin, 1974, 70 pence).

Approach to Quakerism by Edgar B. Castle (QHS, 1961, rptd. 1971, £1.80).

The Amazing Fact of Quaker Worship by George H. Gorman. (QHS, 1973, rptd. 1979, £1.25).

George Fox

The Journal of George Fox ed. by John Nickalls (London Yearly Meeting, 1952, rptd. 1975, *cloth* £6. *paper* £4). Other editions available, differing in completeness.

George Fox and the Valiant Sixty by Elfrida Vipont (Hamish Hamilton, 1975, *cloth* £3.25, *paper* 75 pence).

The Personality of George Fox by A. Neave Brayshaw (Allenson, 1933) Out of print.

George Fox and the Light Within by Rachel Hadley King (Friends Book Store, Philadelphia, 1940) Out of print.

History

The Quakers: their story and message by A. Neave Brayshaw (QHS, 3rd edn. 1938, rptd. 1969, £2).

The Story of Quakerism by Elfrida Vipont (Friends United Press, 1954, rptd. 1977, £3).

The Beginnings of Quakerism by William C. Braithwaite (Sessions, 2nd edn. 1955, rptd. 1970, £8).

The Second Period of Quakerism by William C. Braithwaite (Sessions, 2nd edn. 1961, £8.50).

Margaret Fell: Mother of Quakerism by Isabel Ross (Longmans, 1949) Out of print. A full and interesting study of the co-worker and wife of George Fox, and of her able band of daughters by her first marriage to Judge Fell of Swarthmoor Hall.

Quaker work and witness
Quaker Encounters by J. Ormerod Greenwood (Sessions, 1975-8, 3 vols. £5.50 each). A study of two centuries of Quaker activity in the relief of suffering caused by war or natural calamity.

All the books listed above are obtainable from the FRIENDS BOOK CENTRE, FRIENDS HOUSE, EUSTON ROAD, LONDON NW1 2BJ. A full list of Quaker literature will be sent on request.